THE PLACE OF RELIGION
IN PUBLIC SCHOOLS

THE PLACE OF RELIGION

IN PUBLIC SCHOOLS

A Handbook to Guide Communities

By

VIRGIL HENRY
Superintendent of Schools
Orland Park, Illinois

HARPER & BROTHERS PUBLISHERS NEW YORK

THE PLACE OF RELIGION IN PUBLIC SCHOOLS

Table of Contents

Preface

Leading educators have been telling us for a long time that adequate provision for the wholesome development of children and youth requires cooperative effort by the various community agencies, particularly the home, church, and school. Within recent years many American communities have taken this idea seriously and have been trying to do something about it. The need has been felt in most other communities, but too often the "know-how" has been lacking.

In spite of the tremendous improvements in public education in our generation, evidence from many sources indicates that we are still far short of our ideals. Thoughtful Americans whose messages reach us daily by newspaper, magazine, and radio complain that typical youth—even those in colleges and universities—do not know what they believe in economics, politics, or religion. Students of communism and of other ideologies at work in the world tell us that a basic reason for the strength of these movements is the fact that they have creeds and confessions of faith which their members are required to understand and to practice. We are constantly warned that the only way to meet these faiths is with a faith that is equally strong. The concern of a large majority of our people about this problem is reflected in the results of a recent survey of public opinion on the effectiveness of public education in the United States in which the most frequently mentioned of seven major complaints is the "lack of fundamental character training."

Most religious leaders and many other Americans believe that religion is one of the main sources of morality. Even those who do not urge the acceptance of a particular faith or personal religion often point out the importance of a knowledge of religion as an essential part of a total understanding of the culture. On this subject Justice Jackson of the United States Supreme Court wrote in 1947: "One can hardly respect a system of education that would leave the student wholly ignorant of the currents of religious thought that move the world society for a part in which he is being prepared."

The best public schools have been emphasizing moral and spiritual values for years. They have encouraged the development of kindness, fair play, democracy, and other worthy qualities. Such emphases are important and should be continued and strengthened. But many educators and religious leaders feel strongly that the *practice* of these highly desirable qualities should be accompanied with more attention to an *understanding* of why they are important. The Committee on Religion and Education of the American Council on Education studied this problem for three years and published its conclusions in 1947. This committee recommends that public schools experiment with an objective "study of religion" as a part of the culture (in contrast to the "teaching of religion," which to many people implies sectarian indoctrination) as one means of developing among youth a knowledge of the "faiths men live by." The public school aim would be to make youth religiously literate, while the sectarian goal of leading them to accept a particular faith would continue to be the sole responsibility of the home and the church or synagogue.

I believe that this recommendation is worthy of serious consideration by responsible leaders in American communities. At the same time, I feel that most local leaders who are interested in this proposal are likely to need practical guidance on *how to do the job*. This handbook is an attempt to meet that need. It should be of interest to school administrators and teachers and to professional and lay leaders in religious and other character-building community agencies.

The study out of which this book grew was my major project for the degree of Doctor of Education at Teachers College, Columbia University, conferred in 1948. I wish to acknowledge my indebtedness to the educational and religious leaders whose cooperation and encouragement made this work possible.

I am particularly grateful to the three members of my project committee: Professor Harrison S. Elliott of Union Theological Seminary, and Professors F. Ernest Johnson and John K. Norton of Teachers College.

Almost daily during my work on this project I discussed it with graduate students who were interested, and I often found their suggestions extremely helpful. Of these students I am especially indebted to Mr. L. Howard Grimes, Mr. Walter Holcomb, and Mr. C. Gratton Kemp.

Some of the most valuable assistance came to me by mail from more than three hundred educators and religious leaders with whom I corresponded. Many of these persons sent me copies of their courses of study, curriculum guides, and school bulletins; and others wrote long letters describing and evaluating the practices in the institutions which they represent. This kind of help enabled me to study and to include in my report many practices considered successful in a fairly large number of public and private schools throughout the country. I acknowledge this generous cooperation with thanks.

The kindness of individuals and of publishing companies

in permitting me to quote personal letters and copyrighted materials simplified my work and added emphasis to many points of view expressed.

Also, I am grateful for the financial assistance provided by the United States government under the "G. I. Law." Without this aid it is unlikely that I should have found it possible to stay in school.

Finally, I wish to acknowledge the cooperation and encouragement of my wife, Ruby Worrell Henry, during these years of graduate study. In order that I might achieve this goal she has worked long hours daily, at the same time willingly enduring the inconveniences of student life in crowded quarters in New York City.

May, 1949   VIRGIL HENRY

THE PLACE OF RELIGION
IN PUBLIC SCHOOLS

Introduction

Are Americans losing their moral standards? Those who answer this vital question in the affirmative cite evidence of moral confusion in our time. They say, for example, that few Americans know what they believe. Surveys indicate that many young people are groping for spiritual insight, often without much success. The public schools are accused of failing to teach children either how to think or what is worth thinking about. The home, the church, and the synagogue admit their inability to cope with the situation alone. In 1944 Laski wrote of modern civilization: "Almost as clearly as in the declining days of the Roman Empire our scheme of moral values seems to have broken down."[1]

However, there is evidence on the other side too. In discussing this question in a Town Meeting of the Air radio broadcast, Oxnam reminded his audience of the "mines in England a hundred years ago—women hitched to ore cars, dragging them along the levels toward the shaft; children going below ground on Monday morning and not coming up until Saturday night,"[2] and he concluded that at least in this phase of moral behavior we are making progress. He found encouragement, also, in what he described as the moral sensitivity of American youth "on the question of war and the necessity of establishing world law and order, and a similar alertness on social justice and racial brotherhood."[3] In his opinion, it is a good sign when one finds college youth more interested in abolishing "Jim Crow" cars than in hearing "pretty preachments about brotherhood."[4]

While spokesmen for these two points of view may disagree on the direction in which we are moving, they are united in the conviction that our present moral status leaves something to be desired; and both seek ways to bring about improvements. This search requires a consideration of the sources of moral value, and on this subject also opinions differ. While some people argue that goodness has its roots in the mysteries of faith in God and others contend that virtues are developed through human effort alone, a third group insists that the "sources of moral value are multiple, not singular."[5] Of these multiple sources, says this latter group, religion is one, but only one. Lindeman writes:

When, for example, I survey my own life from this value viewpoint, I discover that my sense of the right, the true, the beautiful, the just and the good has been nourished by many springs. I find my values have been taken from religion, from science, from ideologies, from secular philosophy, from literature, the arts and from my ongoing experience.[6]

Among those who blame our public schools for many of today's problems, one writer expresses his opinion as follows:

Our forefathers believed that education necessarily produced better people. Their kind of education did.

Materially, our 2½-billion-dollar-a-year educational system is the most impressive school establishment in history. Morally, the little red schoolhouse was a better investment.[7]

Lindeman holds a different view on the effectiveness of public education. He says,

. . . I honestly believe that, were realistic tests available, we would discover that sounder moral teaching now takes place in public schools than in any other American institution, churches included. Unhappily, however, the practice is not widespread, and is left largely to chance.[8]

Not all those who doubt the success of the church in meeting the problems in our time are laymen. Theologian Niebuhr, for example, says that the Protestant churches in America have often been guilty of attempting to dodge real issues by emphasizing "a scrupulous legalism, expressed in extravagant rules of Sabbath observance and a prurient attitude toward sex problems."[9] He states that Protestantism has steadily lost influence in the past hundred years and suggests as one reason the fact that the kind of religion which it has often stressed is "thin." He says that many a church of yesterday, "where a Gospel of repentance and faith was preached with power, has become today a kind of community center where a simple moralism is preached, not much higher than the prudential virtues which constitute the creed of a Rotary club."[10]

While some try to show that either the public school or the church is largely responsible for unsatisfactory moral standards, others seem equally certain that the fault lies mainly with the home; and their arguments are often convincing too. Perhaps it is nearest the truth to say that we are all involved in the problem and only through wise planning and action can we reasonably hope for much improvement. In suggesting a community approach to the problem of character education Dimock writes:

It is not enough to have representatives from the schools, churches, and social agencies in these community-planning councils. The functional interests in the community—political, business, industrial, labor, the professions—must be represented if the total way the community functions is to be oriented to ethical human values. The precinct captain may be more influential than the school or church school teachers; likewise, the labor leader, the movie manager, the plant foreman, the business executive may influence more patterns of community behavior than leaders in "character" education.[11]

If Dimock's reasoning is sound, it would be both unfair and unrealistic to expect the public schools to accept all or even most of the responsibility for unsatisfactory moral behavior. At the same time, the public schools are perhaps in a better position than any other institution to initiate planning and to undertake programs which could ultimately result in coordinated effort by the many groups and individuals upon whom real improvement should depend. Any serious attempt in this direction by the public schools would undoubtedly involve attention to religion.

Many leading Roman Catholics, Protestants, and Jews believe that secularism is a basic cause of the world's ills. A complete understanding of secularism in contemporary America is possible only if one traces the consistent tendency in the Western world since the later Middle Ages to separate religious faith and institutions from business, politics, and economics. Thus, many secularists in our time do not deny religion but rather look upon it as irrelevant to the problems of everyday living. The more extreme secularists, however, set forth their beliefs as a philosophy of life which takes the place of religion, making religious creeds and institutions unnecessary.

While this secularization of American life provided a background for the elimination of formal religious instruction from the public schools more than a century ago, it was not the immediate cause. Neither did this action result from the provision in the Constitution of the United States that "Congress shall make no law respecting an establishment of religion, or prohibiting the free exercise thereof."[12] This step was taken only when conflicts among various sects in the same communities grew out of the attempt by each to use the public schools as a means of indoctrinating the pupils in its own particular beliefs. It was this struggle which caused Horace Mann to lead the movement to combat sectarian religious instruction in tax-supported institutions. A law to this effect was passed in Massachusetts in 1827, and the principle gradually spread throughout the country. The courts have generally held that while religion may be studied in the public schools, sectarian indoctrination must be avoided.

Those who believe that secularism is responsible for much of the chaos in the world today are constantly searching for ways to make religion a vital force in the lives of more people. Such persons favor doing everything possible to strengthen the religious activities in the homes, churches, and synagogues, and many of them would like to find a way, without violating the principle of the separation of church and state, to enable children to study religion in or in close connection with the public schools. Of the various methods which have been proposed and to some extent are being tried, the following are perhaps the most deserving of attention:

1. *The "released-time" plan.* By this plan the public schools release pupils for one or more hours each week upon the request of their parents to allow time for instruction by teachers of religion. The cost is met by the cooperating religious groups. This method is in operation in some 3000 American communities. Closely related to it is the "dismissed-time" plan by which all the pupils in the school are dismissed during the time scheduled for religious instruction, instead of only those pupils who are actually enrolled in the courses.

2. *Public support of parochial schools.* Such a plan is in operation in several European countries. In the United States

it would mean that while the public schools would continue to exist, each community would also have parochial schools for all religious groups requesting them. The state would require certain general standards to be met, and then public taxation would be used to support all approved schools.

3. A *"common core"* of *religious beliefs*. Some people say that since Roman Catholics, Protestants, and Jews insist upon similar standards of ethical conduct and have certain beliefs in common, as faith in the Old Testament, one God, and prayer, it is possible and desirable to teach this "common core" of religion in the public schools.

4. An *objective study of religion as a part of the culture*. The adoption of this proposal would mean either the addition of special classes in religion or the integration of religious subject matter at places where it seems naturally to belong in the various subjects already included in the curriculum. Of these two methods of studying religion objectively, probably most educators would prefer the latter, particularly in the elementary and secondary schools. In teaching history, for example, the part that religion has played in shaping the ideas of the culture would be presented; in teaching literature the great religious classics, including the Bible, would be read; in sociology the churches and synagogues would be studied just as other institutions in the community. Similarly, religion would be considered wherever it seems to fit naturally into the sciences, music, art, and drama. The aims would be to make youth religiously literate and to help them to come to grips with real moral and religious problems, but not to lead them to accept any particular faith or personal religion. This latter responsibility, necessarily sectarian in nature, would continue to be borne by the home and the church or synagogue.

THE COMMITTEE ON RELIGION AND EDUCATION

In 1944 the American Council on Education, in cooperation with the National Conference of Christians and Jews,
assembled a group of prominent educators and religious
leaders at Princeton, New Jersey, to discuss in an exploratory
manner the relation of religion to public education. Following this meeting the American Council on Education ap-
pointed the Committee on Religion and Education to insti-
gate studies and activities designed to stimulate informed
thinking in this area. This committee, consisting of educational leaders and representatives of the three major faiths
in the United States, issued a report in 1947, under the title
*The Relation of Religion to Public Education: The Basic
Principles.* This report presents the committee's conclusion
that the study of religion as a part of the culture under the
direction of the public schools, the fourth proposal above,
is educationally sound and in harmony with the basic policy
on this subject in the United States. In his foreword the
president of the American Council on Education writes
that it is hoped the principles set forth "will stimulate constructive criticism and experimentation."[13] It is expected that
this report will be followed by more studies and activities
under the guidance of this committee.

To assume, however, that the recommendations of this
Committee on Religion and Education will be everywhere
approved is unrealistic. Furthermore, the opponents of the
proposals will include not only secularists but also many
earnest and thoughtful Roman Catholics, Protestants, and
Jews. These sincere critics of the committee's report will
offer such reasons as the following for their opposition:

1. The introduction of the formal study of religion into
the public schools, regardless of the method employed, is a

violation of the American principle of the separation of church and state.

2. Many of the religious groups all over America will object if the Bible is read in the schools merely as one of the great religious classics. They will insist that it be taught as the Word of God or not at all.

3. To study religion objectively in the schools would necessitate subjecting the religious beliefs and practices of the various sects to open examination and criticism, and many of the religious bodies would bitterly oppose such procedures in the classroom.

4. Few public school teachers are adequately trained to guide children in a study of religion, and those few would be unable or unwilling to avoid sectarian indoctrination. Furthermore, poorly trained teachers of religion, however sincere, could not possibly present the great religious beliefs fairly, and this failure would lead to negative results in the lives of the pupils and to strife in the community.

5. The integration of religious subject matter into practically all parts of the school curriculum would make it impossible to excuse conscientious objectors without removing them entirely from the school.

6. Even if it were possible to include an objective study of religion in the public schools, the results would be negligible. It takes more than facts about religion to change ways of living and behaving. Anything less than personal commitment to and active participation in the programs of churches and synagogues is entirely inadequate.

7. If the public schools were to assume responsibility for making children religiously literate, the actual result would be to weaken still further the moral and religious influence of the home and the church and synagogue, since these institutions would be quick to shift all religious responsibilities to the school.

8. The public schools already emphasize spiritual qualities, such as kindness, cooperation, honesty, and dependability; and it is values of this kind which really count in the development of good character.

A careful study of the 1947 report will make it clear that the committee was fully aware of these problems and many others and that the final recommendations take them into account. Not only does the committee recommend experimentation with an objective study of religion in the public schools in spite of these difficulties, but it insists that any other course of action is a serious violation of the most acceptable philosophy of education. Furthermore, argues the committee, the failure of the schools "to play a part in acquainting the young with the role of religion in the culture while at the same time accepting such responsibility with reference to other phases of the culture, is to be unneutral—to weigh the scales against any concern with religion."[14]

In *The Christian Century* Morrison expands this idea by describing our sound philosophy of education in America but our failure to apply it in the area of religion. The modern theory of education, he writes,

. . . conceives the school as a method of introducing each new generation into the wisdom and values which the community cherishes. Whatever the community holds to be significant in its own life tends strongly to find its way into the pattern in which the teaching profession organizes the curriculum of the school. It is on this principle that the curriculum includes instruction in science, art, economics, politics, history, literature, even business. The curriculum is thus, in theory, a replica in miniature of the common life.

The school sees millions of citizens marching to the polls, and it teaches civics and politics. It sees millions at work in the factories and offices, and it teaches economics and business methods. It sees millions entering galleries where sculptures stand and pictures are hung, and it teaches the history and canons of art. It sees throngs crowding great halls where symphonies and operas and plays are rendered, and it teaches music and drama. It sees all the people living in homes, and it teaches domestic economy. It sees innumerable workers in academic laboratories and technological departments in industry, and it teaches science. It sees its society cherishing great traditions, and it teaches history and literature.

For religion, however, the school has a blind spot. It does not see the millions going to churches. It does not ask why they go, what is in their minds, what they do in church, what literature they read, how their churches are organized, what social concerns engage them, what differences exist among them, out of what history and tradition all this devotion has sprung, what significance this vast phenomenon of religious faith and organization possesses for democracy and culture. To ask these questions and to answer them is forbidden in our educational system. The school does not know that there is such a thing as religion in American society. . . .

Obviously, no one has the right to demand that the schools be used to indoctrinate their pupils in his sectarian beliefs. But this principle applies also to politics and economics and history and many other subjects. Yet the schools do not exclude political science because the community is divided into Republicans, Democrats, Socialists, Communists, and the rest. Nor does it exclude economics because there are capitalists and New Dealers in the community. If these subject matters can be taught without doing violence to partisan prejudices, religion can also be taught without doing violence to the prejudices of Protestants, Catholics, and Jews.[15]

Finally, the committee states its conviction that those secularist educators who insist upon a no-religion-in-education policy and at the same time demand freedom in tax-supported institutions to indoctrinate students against religious beliefs, are strangely inconsistent. In the words of the committee's report, "we could not discharge the responsibility placed upon us in the preparation of this document if we did not declare our conviction that negative religious dogmatism in the schools is as un-American as positive religious dogmatism. Indeed, in the long run it may be more vigorously resented.[16]

THE PURPOSE AND CONTENTS OF THIS STUDY

The purpose of this book is to offer basic guidance to communities desiring to experiment with an objective study of religion in the public schools. Many suppose there are no such places in the United States. Such an assumption is false. The truth is that public school superintendents and teachers in many places, including some of the large cities, have been experimenting in this area for years. Unfortunately, in some instances, an examination of what these schools are doing leads one to suspect that even though the people represented seem to accept the practices that are taking place, there is some question as to whether those in charge have a clear understanding of the meaning of studying religion objectively with the conscious aim of avoiding all forms of sectarian indoctrination. In addition to the work being done in these public schools under the direction of the public school teachers, the 3000 communities in the United States operating "released-time" programs supply further evidence that large numbers of people feel that the homes, churches, and synagogues are unable to offer adequate programs in religious education by the traditional methods alone.

The deep feelings of emotion which so often accompany even the suggestion that the subject of religion in public education be considered, make it easy to understand why many educational and religious leaders prefer to label the whole area as "too hot" to approach. The report of the Committee on Religion and Education is an attempt to get beneath this surface of emotion and look at the problem realistically to determine what is possible and desirable and what is not. The committee makes no effort to conceal the fact that the problem is difficult, and it freely admits "that in all probability there are communities where the situation is so rigid that no innovation could be attempted without a degree of friction that would nullify any gain" that might result from the undertaking.[17] In other communities, also, only certain beginning steps could be taken in the direction of the total program recommended.

In addition to the fact that this subject is normally one of general interest throughout the country, the 1948 decision of the Supreme Court invalidating the "released-time" plan in operation in Champaign, Illinois, makes a reexamination of contemporary proposals and practices with reference to this problem particularly appropriate at this time. Obviously, the Champaign Case cannot be used as a basis for judging the constitutionality of an objective study of religion in the public schools. However, those who favor the plan upon which this project is based will be interested in reading the following quotation from the separate opinion of Justice Jackson, who voted with the majority in the 8-to-1 decision to invalidate the "released-time" plan as practiced in Champaign:

Perhaps subjects such as mathematics, physics or chemistry are, or can be, completely secularized. But it would not seem practical to teach either practice or appreciation of the arts if we were to forbid exposure of youth to any religious influences. Music without sacred music, architecture minus the cathedral, or painting without the scriptural themes would be eccentric and incomplete, even from a secular point of view. Yet the inspirational appeal of religion in these guises is often stronger than in forthright sermon. Even such a "science" as biology raises the issue between evolution and creation as an explanation of our presence on this planet. Certainly a course in English literature that omitted the Bible and other powerful uses of our mother tongue for religious ends would be pretty barren. And I should suppose it is a proper, if not an indispensable, part of preparation for a worldly life to know the roles that religion and religions have played in the tragic story of mankind. The fact is that, for good or for ill, nearly everything in our culture worth transmitting, everything that gives meaning to life, is saturated with religious influences, derived from paganism, Judaism, Christianity —both Catholic and Protestant—and other faiths accepted by a large part of the world's peoples. One can hardly respect a system of education that would leave the student wholly ignorant of the currents of religious thought that move the world society for a part in which he is being prepared.[18]

Included here is an earnest attempt to identify and to clarify the major problems and dangers, some of them very real, which inevitably accompany the suggested experimentation. Local experiments cannot be expected to succeed unless all groups within the community, the secularists as well as the people represented by the various religious faiths, are dealt with objectively and fairly whenever their institutions, beliefs, literature, struggles, and contributions to democracy are studied. This is possible only if indoctrination either for or against religion is scrupulously avoided in the public schools. If the opposite impression seems at times to be implicit in this report, such an effect is unintentional. The fact cannot be emphasized too strongly that the aim is an understanding of religion, not indoctrination.

This project is based upon the assumption that the local leaders accepting responsibility for initiating an experiment in the study of religion in the public schools will need fairly detailed guidance for at least two years: the first year for intensive preliminary study and planning and the second year to launch the actual program in the school, observe it closely in operation, change as necessary the tentative procedures being tried, and set up a more permanent plan for future expansion and improvement if the results seem to justify such action. Following is a summary of the contents of the six chapters in which it is hoped communities will find such guidance:

Chapter 1. *Realism in Planning.* The purposes here are two: first, to examine some of the major difficulties which may hinder the success of the plan; and second, to clarify what it is felt the proposed program can and cannot reasonably be expected to accomplish if undertaken seriously and intelligently by the people of a community.

Chapter 2. *Curriculum Proposals.* No attempt is made to outline the contents of a complete curriculum but rather to offer suggestions which local leaders are asked to consider in their search for subject matter and activities likely to prove meaningful and useful in the particular school concerned. Each school should begin slowly and work hard to make the first innovation succeed before trying a second one, thereby building its own curriculum over a period of years. Such a curriculum would always be subject to change as conditions and needs seemed to require.

Chapter 3. *Matters of Policy.* An effort is here made to point out the importance of democratic participation in policy formation by all groups which will be affected by the program. Attention is given, also, to the use of publicity and to the need for real consensus in contrast to the principle of majority rule. Some typical problems are briefly discussed, not with the intention of solving them, but rather with the aim of suggesting the basic issues that will have to be faced squarely before solutions are possible.

Chapter 4. Selecting and Training Teachers. The following topics are discussed:

1. Special attitudes and abilities desirable in teachers who lead;
2. Motivation of public school teachers to assume leadership;
3. Selection of teachers to lead;
4. The workshop as a method of teacher training;
5. Suggested contents of the first workshop course;
6. Provision for in-service training and supervision.

Chapter 5. Community Preparation. This is an attempt to outline in logical order the essential phases of a program of study, discussion, and action which it is recommended the community should include in preparing itself for the experiment. It is based upon the assumption that one year is the minimum amount of time to be used in preparation for even a small beginning.

Chapter 6. Expansion and Improvement with Experience. This final chapter presents a plan for the reexamination of the whole program during the first year of actual experimentation. Also, consideration is given to the establishment of a permanent community educational council to supersede the special sponsoring committee organized originally to guide the experiment in its beginning. Such a permanent council would undertake long-range planning to coordinate and improve the total effectiveness of all the educational agencies in the community.

Finally, the fact should be stated that this project has been carried out independently of the American Council's Committee on Religion and Education.

I Realism in Planning

Proposals for the improvement of our schools are useful only if they are both educationally sound and practically possible. Unfortunately, educational theorists do not always take both phases of this requirement into consideration. Also, the sponsors of an innovation in educational practice sometimes advance their particular scheme as the answer to a range of problems too broad to be solved by any single method. Then, when the application of the proposal fails to accomplish everything that has been claimed for it, the tendency among observers is to label the whole idea as unsound. In order to avoid a misunderstanding now which might lead to an inaccurate evaluation later, this initial chapter attempts: first, to examine some of the main implications and dangers of the proposal to include an objective study of religion in the public schools; and second, to indicate as clearly as possible what advantages it is felt a community may expect to derive from its adoption.

SELECTION OF COMMUNITY FOR EXPERIMENTATION

The degree of success likely to characterize the proposed experimentation will depend to a great extent upon the attitudes of the people in the community in which the attempt is made. If the religious sects are as uncompromising today as their predecessors were a century ago, obviously the results

16

now will be no better than those achieved by different methods and for other purposes then. While it is true that as late as 1815 religious instruction in the schools was the accepted practice, this was a time when the religious life in America was weak and in most communities there was a homogeneous population. In the first half of the nineteenth century both of these conditions changed. The religious revival which started in England under the leadership of Wesley spread to America and during the years 1800–1850 multiplied by ten the church membership in this country. During the same period many new Protestant sects appeared and Jewish and Roman Catholic immigrants from Europe helped to diversify the population. Bitter antagonisms developed among the Protestant sects, and anti-Catholic prejudice led to violence more than once.

As the country grew and developed, it became clear that the extension of state-supported education was a necessity in order to prepare the people for the responsibilities of citizenship in the democracy. The churches, whose control of education in the past had seldom been questioned, expected to continue this control under public support; but the inability of the many sects to cooperate among themselves made such a plan impossible. The struggle among the sects grew so bitter that it became apparent that a plan would have to be found whereby the public schools would be required to avoid favoring any particular religious group or groups over the others. Through the influence of Horace Mann the Massachusetts Act of 1827 was passed. It required that the school committees should "never direct to be used or purchased in any of the town schools any books that were calculated to favor the tenets of any particular sect of Christians."[1] Other states passed simliar laws, and as new states were admitted to the Union they included provisions to this effect in their constitutions. Thus, this principle became the accepted policy in the United States. While it forbids sectarian indoctrination in the public schools, it does not actually eliminate religion from the curriculum. If the tendency to exclude religion from public education has been the practical result of this policy, the major fault lies in the attitudes of the religious groups rather than in the policy itself. Therefore, whenever the various sects in American communities are willing to permit the schools to study the religions of all without favoring one over the others, such a study should be possible.

While there is ample evidence that many communities are interested in the problem, it is not known whether many of them would be willing to allow the public schools the freedom they would need to work effectively in this area. The answer to this question depends upon the real intensity of sectarian antagonisms today. On this subject Niebuhr is not optimistic. In an article condemning both the Protestants and Catholics for their unreasonable sectarianism he writes:

If two forms of the Christian faith, though they recognize a common Lord, cannot achieve a little more charity in their relations to each other, they have no right to speak to the world or claim to have any balm for the world's hatreds and mistrusts.[2]

A similar attitude is expressed by Lindeman in these words:

But there are three groups of Christians—Roman Catholic, Greek Orthodox, and Protestant, and they do not love one another. Neither are they meek or pacific. Indeed, these Christians, in contradiction to their basic creed, have aggressively exploited the earth and have been among the great war-makers of modern history.[3]

On the other hand, some prominent Americans are more hopeful. For example, Bower thinks that

. . . the sharp lines that once separated the sects have for some time been in the process of decay. The general public and the denominations themselves have less and less interest in the theological differences that had their origin in issues no longer relevant to contemporary life, and the denominations are coming to stress their common convictions and responsibility to society.[4]

And finally, Morrison feels confident that

. . . there are countless local communities whose religious homogeneity is such that they would gladly open their schools to the experimentation which must necessarily precede the universal introduction of religious instruction in public education. When it is once demonstrated that religion can be taught in a manner acceptable to Catholic, Protestant, and Jew, yes, and to that portion of the community which is not attached to any sect, the problem will be potentially solved.[5]

These expressions of opinions present two possible answers to the question as to what standards should be used to judge the suitability of a community for experimentation, and both possibilities are important. The first is suggested by Morrison's statement that initial experiments should be undertaken in places that are fairly homogeneous from a religious point of view. It seems obvious that there will be fewer initial difficulties if this suggestion is followed, but there is also the danger that the leaders may tend to use materials favoring the particular faith which most of the local adults accept. To yield to this temptation would not only result in failure to test the validity of the theoretical plan but would also mean the partial denial of religious freedom to any minority groups affected. The second possibility is to find communities which are religiously heterogeneous and which are also willing to make the sacrifices necessary to go all the way as pioneers in this educational development. To some groups the price required may seem high, but the results should be most satisfying. The opportunities are particularly challenging in these communities in which the religious differences are great.

Leaders contemplating experimentation in either type of community should be very sure to consider realistically the dangers and opportunities in their particular locality before proceeding further with the plan. Probably the best way to make certain that this step has been taken is to ask for frank expressions of opinion from the representatives of many local groups, including all the religious groups to be affected. In the words of the Committee on Religion and Education, ". . . there should be a meeting of the minds among religious leaders in the community before a school administration can be expected to move in the direction we have indicated."[6]

RELIGIOUS EDUCATION AND THE GOOD LIFE

It is difficult to make a preliminary estimate of the contribution that a study of religion in the public schools would make to better ways of living and behaving. Those who discuss the question often express opinions on this aspect of the subject, but most of what they say has not been verified. Any serious attempt to find the correct answer must include a consideration of the kind of educational procedures that would be used in the plan and also a comparison of the probable effects of knowing and of practice in doing, on qualities of character.

Two possible methods of instruction are available to teachers of controversial subjects. The first involves the idea of setting up in the teacher's mind what he considers to be the desirable outcome and then building a program designed to reach that goal. Such a goal might be democracy or fascism or fundamentalist Protestantism—or anything else. This is the method of indoctrination. The second approach to teaching controversial issues requires an honest and fair examination of all points of view with the purpose of helping the pupils to make up their own minds. Admittedly, this kind of teaching is not easy. It includes presenting the cold facts, but it goes further. It seeks earnestly to lead pupils into the thinking of each group—to enable them both to understand and to feel why certain beliefs and practices are so important to its members. It scrupulously avoids all methods, both direct and indirect, of caricaturing others. It carefully distinguishes between facts and opinions, and welcomes thoughtful disagreements when the latter are involved. As a part of this method the teacher may strive to impress upon the members of his class the importance of taking a stand on an issue, but he carefully avoids any attempt to tell them what stand they should take.[7] It is clear that in guiding the pupils in a study of religion in the public schools only the latter of these two methods can be tolerated, even though some people would contend that only the former would have a positive effect.

Although it is difficult to speak with assurance as to how much an understanding of various opinions of what is good affects ways of behaving, the evidence is strong that mere information about the Bible and religion does not necessarily result in more desirable conduct.[8] If, however, the actual practice of high standards of behavior is accompanied by a thoughtful consideration of why such standards have been regarded as good through the years, there is reason to believe that the intellectual part of the total experience, as well as the practice in doing, has a positive effect. Indeed, in the case of religious practices, such basic understanding seems imperative, since otherwise religious faith may lead to disastrous results. On this subject Fosdick writes:

Religious faith, like any other tremendous power, is terrific in its evils when it goes wrong. Men, under its subtle and prevailing influence, have waged bloody wars, worshiped with licentious rituals, carried on pitiless persecutions, and in bigotry, cruelty, and deceit have grown worse than they would have been with no religion whatsoever. And men, in its inspiring light, have launched missionary movements, founded great philanthropies, built schools, hospitals, orphanages, and in sacrifice, courageous service, and hope of human brotherhood have made man's history glorious. Religion needs intelligence to save it from becoming a ruinous curse; like all power of the first magnitude it is a disaster if ignorantly used.[9]

Probably there is never a more opportune time to study and discuss moral and religious issues than during the high school years in the lives of youth. In the opinion of the authors of *Education for ALL American Youth*:

1. "The adolescent is a questioning person."[10] He wants to get beneath the surface of social customs and understand the basic principles out of which acceptable practices grow.

2. "Adolescence is a period of moral conflicts. . . . At such times boys and girls need help in finding . . . ideals which are compelling in their appeals, and which will guide them" in solving their problems.[11]

3. "Adolescence is a period of searching for life's purposes."[12] It is during these years that choices determining courses for a lifetime are often made—choices of education, marriage, and vocation.

4. For many a youth, "adolescence is a period of dissatisfaction with the world as it is."[13] He sees wars, poverty,

prejudice, and injustice about him, and he wants to remedy these evils.

5. Probably most adolescents have in their minds a good many questions about the meaning of life.

They may not think about them often, but when they face some moral crisis or some tragic experience, these questions become of commanding importance. They are the age-old questions: "What is man?" "Whence does he come from and whither does he go?" "Why should the righteous suffer?" "Are all our human strivings and ideals part of some greater plan, or are they just an accident on a tiny bit of cosmic dust?" "What is worth living for?" "What is worth dying for?"[14]

If these statements about adolescents are true, most people would agree that the school has an obligation to help guide them toward satisfactory answers. And in this task many think there should be a place for a study of the answers which religion offers to these questions even though there is uncertainty as to the actual effect of such study on the lives of the learners. Williams insists that a knowledge of religion is important, "not because it is needed to make men religious —they are incurably so—but in order that they may not fall into the hands of superstition and magic, or of demagogues from the right or the left, but may benefit by the experiences of the human race."[15]

Those who oppose the study of religion in public education often say that the supporters of such a practice:

1. Insist that the Bible "be studied not as great literature but as revealed religious truth";[16]

2. Believe that the process of studying the Bible and other religious materials in the schools would automatically reduce crime and juvenile delinquency;[17] and

3. Really hope to find a way in the plan to indoctrinate pupils in the beliefs of a particular faith.[18]

It is possible that some of the people who want to include a study of religion in the public schools are thinking along these lines, but the report of the Committee on Religion and Education makes it clear that the authors of this document reject such ideas as strongly as do those who oppose any change in our present system. Nor does the committee contend that the study of religious subject matter would inevitably result in better moral behavior of the pupils. Rather, it believes that such study is a necessary part of a school program designed to develop an understanding of the total culture of which religion is an important part. The actual effect of this study on the lives of the children and youth would depend upon the degree to which they made intelligent use of the information acquired. On this subject Morrison writes:

It may be said that this kind of instruction in religion would still be secular—its end would be knowledge about religion, not religious devotion. This is partly true . . . but there are moral and spiritual by-products which flow from a common participation in the pursuit and possession of knowledge.

The possession of knowledge about religion will not, of course, guarantee religious faith and devotion. Neither does knowledge about civics guarantee that one will vote right. Both invest their possessor with the intelligence upon which commitment and action may be based.[19]

MORAL AND SPIRITUAL VALUES IN EDUCATION

As has been indicated, the purpose of this book is to help guide communities desiring to experiment with a study of religion in the public schools. Such an innovation is necessary not only to give youth a true picture of the culture but also to add meaning to those practices emphasizing moral and spiritual values which already characterize the best schools all over America. Gans tells the story of a fifth grade class in which the children discussed with their teacher a radio program heard during Brotherhood Week. She writes:

After they drew the general conclusion from the discussion that an individual should be regarded for what he can do and what would be best for him, one child asked, "If that is so in sports and in hiring workers, shouldn't we have that in our school? Why are Negroes not coming to this school, and why don't we have any Negro teachers?" Education is one piece. It cannot be moral in some ways and at the same time keep these moral influences sealed off from permeating other areas.[20]

. In other words, in effective education knowing and doing go hand in hand. The two cannot be separated without weakening the total effect. Therefore, although the main emphasis here is on the study of religion rather than on those activities which stress moral and spiritual values, there is no intention of minimizing the importance of the latter. They are so essential, in fact, that it would be completely unrealistic to expect positive results from a study of religion in a school in which such activities were not being constantly emphasized. For this reason, sponsors of the proposals in this project should do everything possible to encourage schools engaging in experimentation to work simultaneously to improve their present methods of developing moral and spiritual values. Because these two phases of a satisfactory program cannot be separated, perhaps a brief statement should be made at this time about the meaning of such values, what some of them are, and the methods by which they are already being cultivated in the best schools.

Childs uses the word *spiritual* to mean "those ways of

living and thinking which undergird and contribute to the dignity and worth of human personality. Nothing that degrades the life of the individual man can be considered spiritual; nothing that enriches it can be considered unspiritual."[21]

We learn these ways of living and thinking in the same way that we learn anything else—by thoughtful practice, and the public schools should do everything possible to make such practice the normal procedure. The opportunities for these experiences are present in almost every school situation: in all the subjects of the curriculum, in problems involving pupil conduct, in the guidance program, and perhaps most of all in the day-to-day relationships among the teachers and pupils. "One person, after 30 years, still responds to the challenge of the teacher who said, 'John promised to do this for us and you know that if he promised, he will do it.' "[22] Also, the school can do a great deal to improve the community environment by working closely with families through parent-teacher associations, by cooperating with the religious and other character-building organizations, and by programs of adult education.

No two persons use the same language to describe the moral and spiritual values which public schools strive to cultivate, but the following list of ten includes the ideas most commonly expressed by educators who discuss the subject:

1. *Sense of personal worth.* The school treats each pupil as an individual, striving to provide for him the particular experiences which his needs require. Since no two children have identical needs, the school setup which necessitates the same treatment for all is unsatisfactory.

2. *Delight in fair play.* This goal is stressed in the classrooms and in sports and other activities in all good schools.

3. *Integrity of thought and action.* Numerous experiments indicate that the schools which succeed best in developing integrity are those which strive to eliminate the rewards for dishonesty. They discourage certain kinds of competition among pupils, and they invite honest expressions of opinion even when this means disagreement with the teachers and the administration.[23] In teaching science, "precise information gained is valuable, but even more valuable is the training in honest dealing with facts, no fudging of sums in the laboratory, the disinterested love of supreme truth."[24]

4. *Satisfaction in achievement.* The thrills which come from clear insight and creative thinking occur most often in schools in which the interests of the pupils are carefully studied.

Interest is the phenomenon that indicates growth. Just as friction generates heat, learning generates interest. We don't teach to get interest, but when we don't get interest our teaching isn't prospering. Interest is an index of where the organism is ready to grow. Not all interests need to be followed any more than all limbs on a tree need to be allowed to develop; we select and encourage the limbs that sprout in the desirable places.[25]

5. *Interest in the common good.* This quality develops best in schools that are free from practices creating snobbishness. It is encouraged by all types of activity which make cooperative effort attractive.

6. *Freedom from prejudice.* There seems little doubt that the public schools do more than any other force in America to eliminate prejudice. This is the result of constant intergroup association in work and play. Leading educators are confident that the schools succeeding best in this area are those which provide for the study and discussion of all kinds of controversial issues.

7. *Skill in self-government.* Schools encourage the develop- ment of this ability in pupils by allowing them to act on their own initiative in many things, including the responsibility for vital choices, even though sometimes with disheartening results. Only in this way can children learn to think and act for themselves. The following description of one incident shows what happens when this principle is not understood:

A teacher was once laboriously mixing paints. When asked about having the children do it, she replied, "It's easier to do it myself than to stand over them while they do it." This teacher had not yet learned the art of *standing beside* instead of *standing over.*[26]

8. *Appreciation of beauty.* Pottery, tinted glass, reproductions of great paintings, phonograph records of good music, and other similar materials in the hands of a skilled teacher can create in children a love for beauty which will last as long as they live.

9. *Courage of moral convictions.* Good schools offer their pupils many opportunities to make sacrifices for causes which they believe to be worthy and to oppose whatever they think is wrong. In many schools the pupils are encouraged to organize for cooperative action along these lines.

10. *Faith in the free play of intelligence.* The authors of *The Public Schools and Spiritual Values* have this quality in mind when they discuss "instructional practices which build mechanization or the reverse."[27]

These moral and spiritual values are emphasized through thoughtful practice. In some schools considerable attention is given to practicing them but not much time to consideration of why they are important. The adoption of the proposals here described would certainly strengthen our school programs by helping to remedy this weakness.

DANGERS IN CARELESS EXPERIMENTATION

An examination of the objections expressed by those who oppose experimentation with a study of religion in public education leads one to the conclusion that some of the dangers which they point out are real. Unless the sponsors of the experiments are aware of this fact and understand the seriousness of ignoring it, their efforts, however sincere, may lead to negative results. Among these dangers three require special attention.

The first is the possible tendency of the home and the church and synagogue to shift to the school all the responsibility for the religious education of the young. The Committee on Religion and Education makes it clear that to interpret its report as an encouragement of this tendency is to completely misunderstand the recommendations contained therein. In fact, the committee believes that if the public school succeeds in making youth religiously literate, the task of the home and the church and synagogue will not only be more important than in the past but also far more possible of achievement.[28] This task of the home and religious organizations will include leading children to the acceptance of a particular faith or personal religion and providing the experiences of worship and fellowship required to make that faith meaningful—goals which are sectarian in nature and which cannot be undertaken by the public school. However, unless carefully explained, this division of responsibility between the educational and religious institutions may not always be clearly understood and some parents and religious leaders may be quick to accept any move in the direction of religion in public education to mean that the schools are assuming the total responsibility for the religious growth of children.

To eliminate the possibility of this misconception the

religious and educational sponsors of experiments should work cooperatively from the beginning to clarify in the minds of all the people the limits to which the public schools can go and the specific tasks remaining to the parents and religious leaders. Unless this clarification leads to more rather than less effort by the homes and the religious agencies, the results of the experiments will leave much to be desired.

A second danger to be avoided in the experimentation under consideration in this project is that conditions detrimental to complete religious liberty may be allowed to develop. Freedom of religion means that every person has the privilege of accepting any religious faith that he chooses or, if he sees fit, to deny all religion. If the leaders of experiments adhere strictly to the committee's proposals, it seems unlikely that the principle of religious freedom will be violated. These proposals emphasize repeatedly the basic idea that the public schools should provide the children with an opportunity to study religion objectively, but should carefully avoid all forms of indoctrination. Bower argues in favor of the committee's recommendation when he contends that only in this way will youth be able to understand the culture since, whether one likes religion or not, it "has been and is a part of that culture—a culture which cannot be understood or appreciated when the fact of religion is omitted or obscured."[29] All the children in the public schools, he thinks, even those who are opposed to religion in any form, should study it in exactly the same way that they are asked to study the various economic and political theories whether they agree with any of them or not.[30]

The denial of complete religious freedom occurs, not when all the pupils are asked to study religion objectively, but rather when they are expected to pass beyond this objective study and participate in devotional exercises that may not be acceptable to every religious group represented and certainly not to those who oppose or deny all religion. Even those authorities who insist that they are against any form of religion in public education would do well to reevaluate by this standard such activities as singing Christmas carols and other hymns emphasizing the beliefs of one particular faith, assembly programs and devotional exercises that might not be acceptable to some groups represented, and the required memorization of passages from the New Testament or from a version of the Bible which some of the pupils cannot accept as authentic.

Communities engaged in the proposed experimentation might innocently allow their programs to suffer from one or both of these first two dangers without intending to violate the spirit of the plan. This might easily occur through the overenthusiasm of some sincere leader who does not critically examine the implications of every procedure before putting it into operation. In most instances wise and courageous leaders could correct such errors if they were discovered before antagonisms had developed. The third danger, on the other hand, is likely to appear only if one or more sects in the community deliberately formulate and attempt to put into effect a plan to gain control of the educational system for their own purposes. Any success in this attempt would mean a violation of the American principle of the separation of church and state, the meaning of which should be examined briefly at this point. Weigle writes:

Here in America we believe in the separation of church and state. It is a sound principle, but one which is much misunderstood. It means just what the phrase implies—that church and state are mutually free. It means separation of control, so that neither the church nor the state will attempt to control the other. But it does not mean that the state acknowledges no God, or that the state is exempt from the moral law wherewith God sets the bounds of justice for nations as well as for individuals.[31]

The separation of church and state is not synonymous with a policy of no religion in public education. Nor is it true that the public schools in America exclude all religion even now. What many of them do is to include in their programs various religious practices, unfortunately sometimes sectarian in nature, but fail to adopt a consistent policy designed to give children a basic understanding of the role of religion in the culture. Typical of these religious practices often found in public schools are: Bible reading, simple worship exercises, "released-time" classes in religion sometimes held inside public school buildings, and celebrations of purely religious festivals such as Christmas, Thanksgiving, and the Jewish Hanukkah. Also, in some states public funds are used to supply textbooks and transportation to the pupils in parochial schools.[32]

The church is involved in state affairs in other ways too. Religious bodies often take official positions on social and political issues, and the attitudes of religious groups frequently make themselves felt in political elections. Chaplains serving in the armed forces are paid by public taxation, and religious services are maintained in public prisons and hospitals. Finally, the Bible is used in administering oaths, and presidents and governors issue religious proclamations and set special days for prayer.[33]

What all this means is that complete separation of church and state does not exist in America and never has. As stated above, the important thing to avoid is any condition which would allow either state or church to exercise control over the other. It is imperative that sponsors of plans to study religion in the public schools be alert for possible violations of two basic principles: first, no religious sect should be allowed a position of special privilege with reference to the choice of subject matter, appointment of teachers, or selection of methods of instruction to be used in the public schools; and second, everyone in America is entitled to complete religious freedom.

In addition to keeping alert for signs of these basic dangers, leaders in experiments should keep in touch with representatives of all groups affected. Only in this way is it possible to detect early the existence of minor dissatisfactions which might grow into causes for serious disunity within communities. Suggestions on how to foresee and prevent conflicts will be presented in Chapter 3.

POSITIVE OPPORTUNITIES INHERENT IN THE PLAN PROPOSED

If there is at least partial truth in the many current claims about the moral confusion in this generation, there would seem to be justification for cooperative thinking on the subject by educators and religious leaders. One group of such persons, of course, is the Committee on Religion and Education of the American Council on Education—the authors of the report on which this project is based. These men, all of them outstanding Americans in responsible positions, spent three years in the preparation of this initial report. In the introduction the committee urges Americans everywhere to study the problem, not only to bring about whatever changes seem necessary but also to be in a position to appraise intelligently the proposals that are being constantly advanced on all sides. In the opinion of the committee, if Americans fail to think through the problem carefully and to support sound plans of action it is more than likely that other proposals, some of them "ill-considered and fraught with danger," may gain enough support to create many difficult problems which clear thinking and wise action could prevent.[34]

One advantage, therefore, in studying the committee's report and in cooperating through experimentation in selected communities provided the plan seems to be sound, is to discourage attempts to put into operation any schemes which a careful examination would classify as undesirable or dangerous. Also, a thorough evaluation, by the people, of issues underlying the whole problem would probably result in the elimination or modification of some of the questionable practices already taking place in many public schools throughout the country.

In the second place, any serious attempt to implement the committee's report would automatically remove whatever antireligious effects may have resulted from the public school practice of minimizing the role of religion in the culture. In the following paragraphs Fosdick summarizes a conviction on this subject with which a great many thoughtful Americans are in agreement:

This concern becomes more urgent as the supposed religious neutrality of the public schools from which religion is excluded becomes ever more obviously a fiction. They are not neutral. What our public schools emphasize, or do not emphasize, has a determining effect on what our youths consider important. If, therefore, our schools leave religion out, the negative impression is unmistakable; what can thus be neglected in education cannot be of great significance.

Every year this becomes more manifest as our best schools include in their curricula and extracurricular programs wider and wider areas. If only reading, writing, and arithmetic were taught, the absence of religion would be less noticeable. Now, however, pretty much everything, one way or another, gets into our best schools—sports, music, arts, drama, economics, civics, sociology, psychology, psychiatry, and so on—everything *except religion*.[35]

If religion were studied in the public schools as these other aspects of the culture are studied, the result would be to discourage the present tendency to consider religion as something irrelevant to the problems of everyday living. In the place of this attitude it seems fair to expect that over a period of years there would develop a realization that what religion has to say deserves consideration too. Many people would welcome this innovation in our public educational practices even though it is clear that in the beginning most of the teachers would be inadequately trained. Those who favor such a policy believe that there is less danger in examining and discussing controversial issues freely and openly, even when handicapped by incomplete understanding, than in purposely avoiding subjects on which people hold opposing views.

A third advantage to be derived from a study of religion in the public schools would be the development of religious literacy among the children and youth by giving them a knowledge of religion. Such a knowledge would include: acquaintance with the great religious classics, including the Bible; firsthand contact with the geographically accessible religious institutions and basic information about their past history, present programs, and goals for the future; the main beliefs of the various sects; the major philosophies of life and the attitudes of the different religious groups toward these philosophies; opinions of the great scientists and religious leaders about the relationship between science and religion; and an understanding of the great religious concepts expressed in music, art, and drama.

Almost everyone agrees that an education without this kind of knowledge is incomplete. Many believe, furthermore, that a systematic program in the public schools to develop such a background would lead to a new appreciation of the role of the Judaeo-Christian tradition in the evolution of the democratic way of life. Such a result, they argue, in the degree to which it was achieved, would tend simultaneously to strengthen our democracy and to increase our respect for religion as an influence in history and therefore deserving of our attention today.

There are two final positive results which should come, perhaps mainly as by-products, from the program suggested by the committee. The first is to lift the general level of community living by setting the stage for many new experiences in which moral and spiritual values would get more emphasis. Even though the best schools are already busy in this area, probably none of them are succeeding in doing everything in this respect that can and should be done. Those who look with favor upon the committee's suggestions believe that these proposals offer many opportunities for additional motivation in this direction. Some believe, also, that the stimulus provided by a basic understanding of religion would result in increased church membership and in the kind of religious growth which active participation in such a fellowship can encourage.

The other by-product which should result from the program is greater unity of Americans of all faiths growing out of sincere attempts at sympathetic understanding and appreciation of one another in contrast to mere tolerance. Many public schools are already engaged in intergroup activities which are achieving excellent results, but the need is great, and any new avenues of approach to the problem should be welcome. In a discussion of the ways by which a Protestant teacher can reduce religious prejudice through education, thereby building good will among Roman Catholics, Protestants, and Jews, Howson makes the following statements:

1. A Protestant teacher who is sincerely working through the school to reduce interfaith tensions will generally find Roman Catholic priests and Jewish rabbis friendly and helpful.[36]

2. The classroom atmosphere most suitable for success in such an undertaking is characterized by: freedom and informality, inquiring minds, open and honest consideration and appraisal of all opinions, and absence of the debate as a method of teaching.[37]

3. One of the most helpful procedures is to trace historically how "Roman Catholicism grows out of and is dependent on the Jewish heritage and Protestantism grows out of and is dependent on the Roman Catholic heritage."[38]

4. Another excellent approach is to make a general study of the "common problems of society which have been dealt with by these three groups and to indicate the contributions which they have made to our cultural development."[39]

5. Religious diversity in American democracy is to be expected and its presence can serve to enrich the lives of the people. "The problem is that of reducing . . . tensions to manageable proportions so that they do not disrupt normal social relations."[40]

2 Curriculum Proposals

In many American colleges and universities separate courses in religion are offered. Some believe that if an attempt is to be made to include a study of religion at the elementary and secondary levels of the public schools a similar plan should be employed. Others contend that our school curriculum is already broken up into far too many pieces for effective education and suggest that religious subject matter might better be integrated at places where it naturally belongs in the various subjects already being studied. Surely, that education is best which considers adequately all aspects of the culture, looking at each part as nearly as possible in its natural setting.

The integration of religious materials into the many subjects of the school curriculum is a task certain to require many years. Furthermore, the procedure and results will necessarily vary from one community to another and within the same community from year to year. Some educators and religious leaders would suggest that a functional approach be used in introducing such new subject matter, but only exceptionally skillful teachers could hope to use this method successfully in the beginning. Also, any attempt to make the program directly and immediately functional might lead to a sectarian emphasis, the effect of which would be to defeat the whole purpose of the experiment.

The proposals presented in this chapter are meant to serve only as suggestions in the various areas, not as elements of a specific curriculum recommended for any given school system. Local leaders are asked to examine these possibilities mainly as a means of stimulating their own thinking on the subject under consideration. Having done this, they should then make a survey of the needs, resources, and dangers within their own community and develop their curriculum in the light of their findings. The way should always be left open for revisions as suggested by experience.

In studying this chapter the following basic information should be kept in mind:

First, many of the possibilities presented here are already in use in representative public schools throughout the country and can almost certainly be used in others without danger of creating disunity. Included, also, are some other common practices whose soundness may be questioned.

Second, among these possibilities to be considered are still others which have been used mainly in "released-time" programs and in independent nonsectarian schools and should be attempted in public schools only if it is clear that the people understand them and approve their inclusion in the curriculum.

Third, no attempt is made to limit the suggestions to those materials emphasizing points of view acceptable to all religious groups. Obviously, it is impossible to develop an understanding of the various religious sects without studying their differences as well as the ways in which they are alike. The important thing is that each set of beliefs be presented fairly, objectively, and in a manner which will create respect for persons who sincerely accept those beliefs as basic to the good life.

Fourth, more attention is given to Judaism and Christianity than to other religions because they are more closely associated with the American culture and because information about them is more readily accessible. However, to limit the study entirely to those religions most prevalent in America would result in the pupils' failure to get a proper perspective of the role of religion in the culture, which is the main objective being sought.

RELIGION IN LITERATURE

Although it is recommended that the Bible be used wherever it is needed in the various subjects of the public school curriculum, it will probably be studied most in connection with classes in literature. Justification for major emphasis on this important book is not hard to find.

In 1922 Phelps wrote:

Everyone who has a thorough knowledge of the Bible may truly be called educated; and no other learning or culture, no matter how extensive or elegant, can, among Europeans and Americans, form a proper substitute. Western civilization is founded upon the Bible; our ideas, our wisdom, our philosophy, our literature, our art, our ideals, come more from the Bible than from all other books put together.[1]

Among the many reasons for Bible study discussed in an article in the *Atlantic Monthly,* one contention is, "that passages which at first yield little meaning may later come to life. It is best to treat the book as a mine in which you look for coarse gold in hard rock. Then you go back and work over the discarded material for gold not found the first time."[2]

The authors of *Education for ALL American Youth* put the following words into the mouths of those responsible for the remarkable achievements in the Farmville school:

The Bible contains many great passages which everybody should know and understand. We read them in our courses in literature, as records of the experiences of men of noble spirit and rare insight, seeking answers to eternal questions of right and wrong and the meaning of life.[3]

Finally, the Committee on Religion and Education of the American Council on Education expresses its attitude like this:

The study of the religious classics, not in special religious classes, but in the regular literature program has not been entirely neglected but provision for it is all too inadequate. The English classics are recognized as carriers of our cultural heritage. It can hardly be contested that the Bible is second to none among the books that have influenced the thought and ideals of the Western world.[4]

It must be borne in mind, of course, that in many states there are legal restrictions on the methods of using the Bible in the public schools, and in some communities the attitudes of the various religious denominations may limit the freedom necessary to sound educational practice where the Bible is concerned. These limitations will be considered in later chapters. At this point the proposals will be presented as if such obstacles did not exist.

The integration of religious subject matter into the literature curriculum of the public schools may be undertaken by a variety of methods of which six will be considered briefly in the following paragraphs.

1. *Emphasis on religious values in non-Biblical literature.* Many people believe that numerous selections of literature already being taught in the public schools have deep religious significance which becomes clear when the teachers and their pupils seek honestly to answer the question, What does the

author mean? Desjardins reports the results of a study indicating that many of the objectives of courses in literature as stated by public school authorities are almost identical with the criteria used by religious leaders to determine what constitutes religious values in a poem, song, or story. Among her illustrations which, according to these criteria, contain religious values, are the following patriotic lines by Lanier:

> Long as thine Art shall love true love,
> Long as thy Science truth shall know,
> Long as thine Eagle harms no Dove,
> Long as thy law by law shall grow,
> Long as thy God is God above,
> Thy brother every man below,
> So long, dear land of all my love,
> Thy name shall shine, thy fame shall glow.[5]

Fosdick contends that practically all great literature concerns religious questions, and he illustrates his meaning with *Romola, The Scarlet Letter, Les Miserables, Faust, Othello, Hamlet,* and *Macbeth.*[6] To this list one might add titles indefinitely from the works of such writers as: Chaucer, Milton, Cowper, Burns, Coleridge, Wordsworth, Tennyson, Browning, Eliot, Stevenson, Arnold, Kipling, Carlyle, Emerson, Longfellow, Lowell, Whittier, Bryant, Whitman, Holmes, Markham, Poe, Thoreau, Hawthorne, and many others.

Teachers who want to experiment with emphasizing religious values in literature should have available for reference such helps as *The World's Great Religious Poetry* by Hill,[7] *The Religious Faith of Great Men* by Wallace,[8] *Our Roving Bible* by Nelson,[9] and the "Personal Growth Leaflets," published by the NEA.[10]

2. *Bible study as background for appreciation of English literature and language.* It is difficult to fully appreciate

written and spoken English without a fair knowledge of the
Bible. To attempt to teach literature without reference to
the Bible is unthinkable. Consider, for example, trying to
teach the following lines from Burns' poem "The Cotter's
Saturday Night," which is commonly included in the public
school curriculum, without simultaneously discussing Biblical
materials:

> The priest-like father reads the sacred page,
> How Abraham was the friend of God on high;
> Or Moses bade eternal warfare wage
> With Amalek's ungracious progeny;
> Or how the royal bard did groaning lie
> Beneath the stroke of heaven's avenging ire;
> Or Job's pathetic plaint and wailing cry;
> Or rapt Isaiah's wild seraphic fire;
> Or other holy seers that tune the sacred lyre.
>
> Perhaps the Christian's volume is the theme,
> How guiltless blood for guilty man was shed;
> How He, who bore in Heaven the second name,
> Had not on earth whereon to lay His head;
> How His first followers and servants sped;
> The precepts sage they wrote to many a land;
> How he, who lone in Patmos banished,
> Saw in the sun a mighty angel stand,
> And heard great Bab'lon's doom pronounc'd by
>   Heaven's command.[11]

Or the following prose passage from Lamb's *Essays of
Elia*:

I love a Fool, as naturally as if I were kith and kin to him.
When a child, with childlike apprehension I read those parables
—not guessing their involved wisdom—I had more yearnings
toward that simple architect, that built his house upon the

sand, than I entertained for his more cautious neighbor; I grudged at the hard censure pronounced upon the quiet soul that kept his talent; and—prizing their simplicity beyond the more provident, and, to my apprehension, somewhat unfeminine weariness of their competitors—I felt kindliness that almost amounted to a *tendre* for those five thoughtless virgins.[12]

References to the Bible often appear in newspapers and magazines too. For example, an editorial in the *New York Times* on the subject of accidents in the home includes this statement: "It is the old story as told in the Book of Amos, 'of the man who to escape perils out of doors went into the house and leaned against a wall and a serpent bit him.' "[13]

Finally, persons familiar with the Bible are more intelligent participants in conversations in which a character may be referred to as "a Jezebel" or "a Pilate" or "a Martha" and in which such phrases as the following are used frequently: "the salt of the earth," "a wolf in sheep's clothing," "in the twinkling of an eye," "the grim reaper," "the handwriting on the wall," "casting pearls before swine," "the strait and narrow way," "render unto Caesar," "like David and Jonathan," "to use or hold one's talents," "to bear a cross," "a house divided against itself," "the powers that be," "a mess of pottage," "the widow's mite," "a pearl of great price," "the fat of the land," "all things to all men," and others.[14]

Many public school teachers, therefore, realizing the impossibility of developing an appreciation of the English language and literature without some basic knowledge of the Bible, attempt to present Biblical background incidentally as the need arises.

3. *Correlation of the Bible with literature.* This method is closely related to the preceding one and may be used in schools to clarify the meanings of many selections of literature and at the same time give some attention to a knowl-

edge of the Bible. Typical of the opportunities for such correlation are the following:[15]

a. Hunt's "Abou Ben Adhem" and Luke 10:30-36.
b. Wordworth's "The World Is Too Much with Us" and Matt. 6:22.
c. Milton's sonnet "On His Blindness" and Matt. 11:28-30, 20:6, 25:14-30; Zech. 1:7-11; Eph. 2:8-11.
d. Bryant's "Thanatopsis" and Job 3:2-26; II Tim. 11:28-30; Ps. 139:9.

4. *Reading Bible stories.* Many public schools teach Bible stories, particularly to the younger children. It seems reasonable to believe that this practice could be extended to higher grades, making use of several books already available. Teachers interested in this approach will want to examine the following books: Cohen's *Bible Tales for Very Young Children* (two volumes),[16] Bowie's *The Story of the Bible,*[17] Curtis' *The Story of the Bible People,*[18] Van Loon's *The Story of the Bible,*[19] Fahs' *Jesus, the Carpenter's Son,*[20] Klaber's *Joseph,*[21] Flight's *Moses,*[22] Bowie's *Great Men of the Bible,*[23] and Morton's *Women of the Bible.*[24]

5. *Emphasis on great passages in the Bible.* Only as children begin to develop a real understanding of the Bible by identifying themselves with parts of its message will certain passages take on special significance for them. To encourage such appreciation some educators arrange to have carefully selected passages read aloud repeatedly in school assemblies. Possible selections for this purpose are included in the American Bible Society's "Forty Favorite Chapters in Your Bible."[25] In Louisville, Kentucky, the public school teachers in cooperation with the city Council of Churches are developing a handbook of scripture references for daily read-

ing.[26] In other schools the pupils may be encouraged to form the habit of listening to records and transcriptions of Biblical texts read in dramatic settings. Suggestions of aids suitable for this kind of program may be secured from the Radio Department of the Congregational Christian Churches.[27] Those who prefer to have the pupils make their own choices of the passages to be read frequently should assist them to become thoroughly familiar with Goodspeed's *The Junior Bible*,[28] Sypherd's *The Book of Books*,[29] and other Biblical texts prepared especially for young readers. To compare the Bible with selected scriptures of other great religions *The World's Great Scriptures* by Browne[30] is excellent.

6. *Survey courses on the Bible.* Only pupils of senior high school age can profit much from survey courses on the Bible, and then only if they have in previous years become familiar with many of its parts by the various methods described above. In addition to the Bible itself, some useful references for survey courses are: Browne's *The Graphic Bible*,[31] Chase's *The Bible and the Common Reader*,[32] Goodspeed's *How to Read the Bible*,[33] Goodspeed's *The Story of the Bible*,[34] Atwater's *A Catholic Dictionary*,[35] and *A New Standard Bible Dictionary* by Jacobus, Lane, and Zenos.[36] In the independent Brearley School in New York City the Bible survey course is sometimes introduced by leading the pupils gradually from Greek mythology and history to the legends and history in the Bible. One of the Brearley teachers writes that by this procedure her pupils quickly come to the realization that "the ethics of the Greek gods violate all their ideas of fair play, justice, and dignity, and they end by spontaneously noticing the superiority of the Jewish-Christian conception of God."[37]

RELIGION IN THE SOCIAL STUDIES

The influence of religion in history has been too powerful to allow its elimination from a social studies curriculum designed to develop a clear understanding of today's culture. Furthermore, an examination of representative city and state curriculum guides and courses of study makes it clear that many educators are conscious of the relation of religion to the total culture and that the way is left open for experimentation in this area by the teachers. In most cases, however, specific suggestions to the teachers on how to proceed with such experiments are not offered. In this section six kinds of possibilities will be considered.

1. *Comparative study of religions.* Some attention is given to this subject in many public schools already, but probably in most places the emphasis is slight. Typical of the practices frequently found is a social studies unit in the sixth grade in Louisville, Kentucky, entitled "The Peoples of the Eastern Hemisphere and Their World Relationships." This unit of work gives the children an opportunity to explore several of the great religions.[38] Although this is a beginning, it would seem that additional time and study are needed, preferably when the children are a few years older.

Some suggested references for this kind of experimentation are: Fitch's *Their Search for God*,[39] Baxter's *How Our Religion Began*,[40] Gaer's *How the Great Religions Began*,[41] Braden's *The World's Religions*,[42] Hume's *The World's Living Religions*,[43] Browne's *This Believing World*,[44] and Browne's *The World's Great Scriptures*.[45]

2. *Religion in history.* Opportunities for this kind of emphasis are obvious in many places in both European and American history. In fact, the study of history with little or no reference to religion makes false interpretations inevitable.

In his consideration of this point with reference to the Crusades, Hauser presents an outline from a course of study used in the sixth grade in one of our cities. He notices that the vocabulary of new words and phrases listed for the pupils to learn includes *Crusader, pilgrim, mariner's compass,* and *Renaissance,* but omits *cathedral, monasteries, clergy, Reformers,* and *religion in art.* In his opinion, it is significant that the list ends with the Renaissance. He asks why the Reformation is omitted, and then continues:

The Renaissance is the medieval way of spelling modern secularism. That is to say the Renaissance was not all there was to the Crusades. The Crusades were all that the teacher's guide for Grade Six B says they were, but much more. The Crusades burst forth out of an age that was characterized by a God-centered world view. "God wills it" was the slogan and the spirit of the Crusader.

The rediscovery by the Crusades of the . . . lost knowledge, buried in the literature of the ancient languages, led to a re-examination of religion with a zeal alike in interest and intensity to that devoted to the restudy of human history in general, and the natural sciences. Out of this restudy of the Christian religion came the Reformation, and a revival of religion that led to religious liberty and the other liberties political and individual that have followed and which we treasure so highly today.[46]

Those who are in general agreement with Hauser on the importance of emphasizing the religious aspect of history will be interested in a unit entitled "Transmission of Culture," which is studied by all tenth grade pupils in Montgomery County, Maryland. This unit is divided into four sections: culture, religion, education, and arts. Following is a list of the topics studied under religion:

Cathedrals—Bibles Made of Stone and Glass
The Crusades
The Monks and Monasteries of Medieval Times
Results of the Religious Fervor of the Middle Ages
Crusades Change Home Life of Medieval Europe
Nomadic Religion
Mythology
Superstitions of the Eskimos
Congo Religion
Egyptian Religion
Confucius, a Great Scholar[47]

Many people would agree that this is a step in the right direction even though Hauser's objection to minimizing the importance of the Reformation would apply to this outline also.

In the field of American history, Nall reports some interesting correlation of church history taught in the "released-time" program in Oak Park, Illinois, with the subject matter studied in the eighth grade in the public school. She says that the class was fascinated by the methods used by the different denominations to evangelize the West. In this study they discovered that the public school textbooks gave more attention to the Mormons than to other religious groups, and gradually came to the realization that as a rule it is only when a church becomes a political factor that it is treated by the writers of history texts. To supplement their public school course in this respect they wrote a series of "forgotten pages" in American history. Also, each member of the class made a special study of what the Civil War did to his own denomination. Finally, when the unit on "The Development of the West" was studied in the public school, the "released-time" class did a special project on the influence of the missionaries Jason Lee and Marcus Whitman on the establishment of the Oregon territory.[48]

Another approach to an understanding of the influence of religion in history is through reading well-chosen historical novels and the biographies of such men as Cromwell, Gladstone, Roger Williams, Washington, William Lloyd Garrison, Lincoln, Lee, and Wilson.

Teachers interested in the possibilities mentioned in this section should familiarize themselves with the following books: Smither's *A Picture Book of Palestine*,[49] Bainton's *The Church of Our Fathers*,[50] Desjardins' *Our Living Church*,[51] Manwell and Fahs' *The Church Across the Street*,[52] Hedley's *The Christian Heritage in America*,[53] Sweet's *The Story of Religion in America*,[54] Owen's *Learning Religion from Famous Americans*,[55] and Wallace's *The Religious Faith of Great Men*.[56]

3. *Interfaith education.* Many public schools in America have special programs in operation to develop mutual appreciation and respect in contrast to mere tolerance among the different faiths. Some possible steps toward this goal were discussed briefly at the end of Chapter 1. The following additional suggestions are offered here:

a. Study the role of the church and synagogue in the community in the same way that children and youth in the public schools now study the banks, labor unions, cooperatives, and government agencies. This will require reading in the library, discussion in the classroom, association among the members of the different faiths in cooperative projects, and carefully planned educational excursions to representative churches and synagogues to learn more about what each is actually doing for the betterment of individuals and groups.

b. Visit or read about and profit from the experiences of several public schools which are emphasizing interfaith education, as those in Springfield, Massachusetts, and Los Angeles, California.

c. Study the basic beliefs of the various faiths, particularly the ones represented by the pupils in the school. Probably few public schools in the United States are attempting this, but some of the independent schools are using methods which public schools might consider adopting. In the George School, Bucks County, Pennsylvania, for example, one group of pupils made a study of the "social testimonies and messages of the Protestants, Catholics, and Jews."[57] And the headmaster of the interdenominational Shady Side Academy, Pittsburgh, Pennsylvania, who has worked in interfaith educational programs for years, gives this advice:

Bring out into the open the conflicts between the various faiths and instruct the youngsters in what they are supposed to believe if they are Protestants (Fundamentalists all the way to Universalists) or Jews (Liberal, Conservative or Orthodox) or Catholics. This takes experienced teaching, but it is very important if courses are to be saved from unreality and vagueness.[58]

Some books helpful in interfaith education are: Fitch's *One God: The Ways We Worship Him*,[59] Manwell and Fahs' *The Church Across the Street*,[60] Finkelstein, Ross, and Brown's *The Religions of Democracy*,[61] McCasland's *The Bible in Our American Life*,[62] Eakin's *Getting Acquainted with Jewish Neighbors*,[63] Steinberg's *Basic Judaism*,[64] Landis' *Religion and the Good Society*,[65] Straus' *Religious Liberty and Democracy*,[66] Davidson's *Good Christian Men*,[67] Douglass and Brunner's *The Protestant Church as a Social Institution*,[68] Elliott's *Building Bridges*,[69] and the United Christian Youth Movement's pamphlet *Christian Youth and Interfaith Cooperation*.[70]

4. *Philosophies of life.* Classes in the senior high school

that are interested in going somewhat more deeply into problems of religion and philosophy which have puzzled men throughout the ages will find help in McCasland's *The Bible in Our American Life*,[71] Hyde's *The Five Great Philosophies*,[72] and the series of twelve Hazen Books on Religion.[73] Some of the questions which these books will help to answer are: What is man? What is the meaning of faith? What is the relation of religion to conscience? Is God interested in the human race? What is the meaning of God? How does prayer help people? Why should the innocent suffer?

5. *Religion and contemporary problems.* Other groups in the public school may want to understand better what religion has to say about the many serious everyday problems faced by America and the world in the twentieth century. In this area, too, independent schools have gone further than the public schools. The headmaster of the Brooks School, North Andover, Massachusetts, uses the Bible extensively as a textbook in his social studies classes engaged in studying such problems. He writes:

I believe the point I would emphasize is my increasing personal conviction that the Bible itself serves as the best of all texts, figuratively and literally, for the discussion of all the problems of our world today, whether they be ethical, social, or even economic, and that by using it the Bible itself comes to life and vigor.[74]

In the George School, referred to above, the students study the attitudes of religious bodies on questions of war and peace, international cooperation, and the Ecumenical Movement; and they try to arrive at answers to such questions as the following:

Is it possible to emulate the precepts of the Old and New Testament today, can things still be done "as in the Bible" in this technical age? What is the way out of moral confusion, illustrated in the rising divorce rate? What can be done about the present political machine that seems to know nothing of the high ideals of the church, meeting house, and classroom? Does the desire to live a Christian life exclude a person from the choice of certain vocations?[75]

Suggested references for this kind of study are Eakin and Eakin's Let's Think about Our Religion,[76] McCasland's The Bible in Our American Life,[77] Bower's The Living Bible,[78] Cronbach's The Bible and Our Social Outlook,[79] Kean's Christianity and the Cultural Crisis,[80] Lankard's The Bible Speaks to Our Generation,[81] and Wickenden's Youth Looks at Religion.[82]

6. School cooperation with the religious groups in the community. Many public schools have been active in such cooperation for years. However, there is probably room for improvement in this respect in all communities. Typical of the practices considered desirable in many places are the following:

a. A centralized plan for scheduling activities so that needless conflicts between church and school programs can be avoided.

b. Clear agreements about the possible joint use of certain special equipment, library materials, and rooms for meetings and recreation.

c. Volunteer service by public school teachers in the programs of the churches and synagogues.

RELIGION IN THE PHYSICAL AND BIOLOGICAL SCIENCES

Fosdick describes the conflict between science and religion as "one of the saddest stories ever written" and calls it a "record of mutual misunderstanding, of bitterness, bigotry, and persecution" which wise leadership in both areas might have avoided.[83] The best way to heal the damage already done and to discourage the continuance of this struggle is to help more and more people to understand the respective functions of science and religion. The public schools are in the best position to assume this responsibility. Courses in the physical and biological sciences provide opportunities for pupils to examine simultaneously the contributions of science and religion to the solutions of problems centering around the creation of the universe, the origin and destiny of man, and the nature and purposes of God. When the young are encouraged to study and discuss these questions in the schools, they will gradually come to understand that science and faith need not be in conflict but that science is in fact "based on the assumption of an orderly universe which has to be accepted as a matter of faith."[84] When this time comes, the schools will no longer contribute to the kind of confusion in the mind of the small boy who said to his public school teacher, "If what you say is true, then what my Sunday school teacher said is the bunk."[85]

Perhaps a good place for the schools to start is with stories of the creation of the universe. Only children who are permitted to read the creation myths of many lands in addition to the story in the Bible will be able to make comparisons and draw conclusions of their own. An excellent introductory book on this subject is Fahs' *Beginnings of Earth and Sky*,[86] which supplies children with a background for understanding evolution as a part of God's plan. McKendry writes:

Public school teachers should be prepared to meet questions arising in science. So far it has been left, "If the Bible is true, then science is not true," and vice versa. This is immature on the part of the teachers and confusing to the students. The creation stories of the Bible have a God reference. Should we not give our science stories a God reference too? Can we do it in terms of law, order and beauty?[87]

As the study of the creation stories progresses from the beginnings of land, sea, and sky, to the origins of plant and animal life, attention will be focused increasingly on the theory of evolution. As the pupils become more familiar with the nature of science and of religion, they will tend to minimize the importance of the conflict between the two. In this connection, McCasland says that science is limited to a description of things already in existence. Concerning science he writes:

It cannot tell us where or how these things came into existence. It works with those aspects of the world which can be measured scientifically and tells us many valuable things about them, but it can never tell us the real, ultimate nature of the things with which it deals. To attempt that problem would be to leave the field of science and enter the domain of philosophy and theology. If religious faith keeps its own nature, as well as the nature of science, clearly in mind, it has no cause to feel disturbed by anything that science may discover. Science and religion have in common the belief in an infinite order and to that extent support one another. The scientist can not go beyond that order, but to the religious man it leads to God.

Thus religion believes that man comes from God. It does not deny his kinship to the animal world. Animals too come from God.[88]

The study of the various theories as to the origin of man leads naturally to a consideration of the meaning of life and death. Teachers who wish to examine this subject with their pupils will find help in *Beginnings of Life and Death* by Fahs and Spoerl.[89] This book, written for children of ages nine to fifteen, is divided into two parts: first, "The Scientists' Story of Evolution," and second, "Why Do We Die?" A useful reference for youth of senior high school age is Calhoun's What Is Man?[90]

This kind of emphasis in the science courses in the public schools will necessarily include an attempt to understand the nature of God. Hauser insists that it is the duty of the schools to pass on to children those concepts of God which "fit into the noblest religious interpretations of devout and learned teachers and scientists."[91] One approach to this task may be made by associating God with many examples of law and order in the universe and with the wonder and beauty of nature. Stevens' two books, Child and Universe[92] and How Miracles Abound,[93] will be useful in this undertaking. The children in the week-day religious education program in Oak Park, Illinois, used such a plan in their unit of work entitled "The Universe and I," and the director is considering a similar unit on "The Dark Spots in Life."[94]

Finally, high school students who have spent several years in schools in which the study of religion is provided for, may want to follow the example of a group of seniors in the George School who studied the biographies of leading scientists "with reference to their religious beliefs and the relationship between science and religion."[95] Also, in some communities the educators and religious leaders might consider offering courses to adults designed to lead them in a short time through a program of study and discussion comparable to the one requiring many years in the public schools.

Besides the books already mentioned, the following should also be made available to teachers and pupils engaged in the study of religion as a part of the courses in the physical and biological sciences: Hauser's Latent Religious Resources in Public School Education,[96] the Martin and Judy series,[97] Baxter's How Our Religion Began,[98] Eakin and Eakin's Let's

Think about Our Religion,[99] Munkres' *Which Way for Our Children?*[100] Wickenden's *Youth Looks at Religion,*[101] Sherrill's *The Opening Doors of Childhood,*[102] Hill's *The World's Great Religious Poetry,*[103] and Macmurray's *The Structure of Religious Experience.*[104]

RELIGION IN MUSIC, ART, AND DRAMA

It is generally assumed that frequent contact of children with great music, art, and drama in the public schools inevitably has moral and spiritual effects whether such results are intended or not. Also, some educators feel that there are important character training possibilities, particularly in the "role playing" aspect of school dramatics, and others see a means of the development of group-mindedness in children's working together in teams to create and present dramatic productions. That similar values are claimed for music and art is obvious from a glance at the objectives as stated in courses of study and curriculum guides used in representative public schools. Indeed, some of these objectives are so stated that one wonders if public schools, even though unintentionally, are actually attempting sectarian religious indoctrination through some of their activities in this area. In this section a summary of typical school practices will be presented. A consideration of the possible dangers involved will be included in Chapter 3.

Authorities in some schools indicate that they include religion as an aspect of their music, art, and drama only to the extent that it must be included to develop a complete understanding of the culture. Basically they are in agreement with Bower when he writes that "it is quite impossible to

understand the art and literature of the Western world apart
from religion. Religion has furnished the motif for a large
part of the painting, sculpture, architecture, and music. . . .
Over the centuries the influence of religion has been comparable with that of science, technology, and politics."[105]
They insist that they do not use the study of religion as a
means of urging children to become religious. One committee of principals and teachers puts it like this:

The committee has unanimously agreed that . . . we should
make certain that every child knows certain passages of religious
literature, a selected group of religious songs, and pictures which
are accepted as a part of the cultural heritage of all educated
people.[106]

This committee then lists certain hymns and pictures for all
children to "know" by the time they finish the sixth grade.
Some of the hymns are: "Come Thou Almighty King," "O
Worship the King," and the "Doxology (Old Hundredth)."
The pictures listed include several Raphaels, Watts' "Sir
Galahad," Hoffmann's "Christ in the Temple," and da
Vinci's "Last Supper."

Many educators would give the same reason for asking
children to study the religious works of Handel and Bach,
sing Christmas carols, and understand the religious aspects
of Negro spirituals and our national hymns.

Educators in a second group of schools freely admit that
they hope their emphasis on the religious aspects of music,
art, and drama will encourage religious behavior in children;
but they insist that everything they do is nonsectarian in
nature. Examples of this attitude may be found in Louisville,
Kentucky, and in Los Angeles, California.

In Louisville the music program in the junior high schools
is built around fourteen "centers of interest," of which wor-

ship is one. The assumption seems to be that worship is a normal activity in the lives of the people and therefore the school should provide opportunities for study and practice in this experience. The music suggested for this purpose is divided into five classifications: Christmas music, Thanksgiving hymns, Easter music, hymns, and oratorios.[107]

In Los Angeles the public schools emphasize twelve "key qualities," including faith and reverence. With respect to faith, the objectives are the development of faith in oneself, faith in one's fellowman, faith in our country, faith in the future, and faith in God. The following paragraph headed "Faith in God," is in the syllabus:

Our boys and girls need to understand that no life can be complete without faith in God. We may not all define God in the same terms; but at least we can agree that faith in God means faith in a power greater than ourselves, and that is the important thing. The sages tell us that God is a God of law and a God of love; if we accept Him as such and have true faith, then, whatever happens to us personally, we can say, "Thy will be done."[108]

Among the methods suggested for achieving this objective are listening to music and singing. The music recommended for listening includes: the Negro spiritual "Deep River," Bach's "I Call Upon Thee," and parts of Wagner's *Lohengrin*. Some of the suggestions for singing are: "And the Glory of the Lord" from Handel's *The Messiah*, Mendelssohn's "Lift Thine Eyes," "Faith of Our Fathers," and "Joshua Fit De Battle of Jericho."[109]

A third kind of religious goal sought through music, art, and drama in some schools is the appreciation of other peoples at their best. The particular works selected for this purpose may or may not be religious within themselves. The

Louisville public schools have this as one of their aims in emphasizing Latin American and Russian music.[110] Likewise, people everywhere develop a finer appreciation of the Negro race as they come to understand the meaning of Negro spirituals which, according to Maus, "possess a distinctly religious character, and grow out of a deep yearning of the Negro to understand God and to be reconciled to the hardness of his lot."[111] Similar possibilities exist, of course, in the use of the various kinds of art.

Finally, a fourth procedure is followed in some schools to utilize music, art, and drama for religious purposes. This is an elective plan which is often sponsored on an extracurricular basis, although it may be done as a phase of the regular work of a class. Typical of the activities which some groups might like to consider are:

1. To write a litany for a special program, as commencement.

2. To write and present a play emphasizing the religious qualities in the character of a great person, as Lincoln.

3. To present to the public a play selected for its religious values. Some excellent selections are in Eastman's *Ten One-Act Plays*.[112]

4. To form a radio club to enjoy religious music and dramatics included in broadcasts. The activities of such a group might consist of selecting the best programs, meeting together to hear and discuss them, and systematically encouraging others to listen.

5. To organize groups of singers, prepare religious selections for presentation to the public, and offer services to local organizations.

6. To form a club to visit, study, and discuss great works of art.

RELIGION IN ASSEMBLY PROGRAMS

One of the most controversial issues in the whole question of the relation of religion to public education concerns programs in school assemblies. The arguments on both sides will be considered later. The purpose of this section is to examine some of the practices: first, the more unusual ones, and then those more typical of the average school.

1. *Assembly programs utilizing religious materials selected mainly to further moral and religious growth in children.* A carefully developed plan of this kind has been in use for several years in the Brady Elementary School, Detroit, Michigan. This plan is clearly outlined in a pamphlet entitled *Brady School Plan for Character and Citizenship Training.*[113] The central ideas around which the Brady program grows are presented first in school assemblies, and then teachers are encouraged to develop them further in their classrooms. There are ten of these central ideas or topics, one for each month of the school year. They are: obedience, cooperation, gratitude, love, thrift, industry, gift of speech, beauty in life, trustworthiness, and courtesy.[114] The pamphlet developed by the Brady School faculty includes the following six kinds of help on each topic:[115]

a. Points for informal discussion (to be developed in the classrooms).
b. Prayers for the month (always nondenominational).
c. Hymns to be sung at school assemblies.
d. Poems suitable for memorization.
e. Seasonal and patriotic songs for assemblies.
f. Bibliography.

Typical of the prayers recommended is this one for use by the older children:

Each day I pray, God, give me strength anew,
To do the task I do not wish to do,
To measure what I am by what I give.
God, give me strength that I may rightly live.[116]

Among the "Suggested Things to Do" is the following:

December—the month of Holidays—Discuss the history and religious customs of Hanukkah—the Festival of Light; Christmas—the Christian Feast Day celebrating the birthday of Christ, the Light of the Christian World.[117]

Some of the hymns for school assemblies are: "Come Ye Faithful People," "Prayer of Thanksgiving," "Holy! Holy! Holy!" "Hymn of Peace," "Abide with Me," and "For the Beauty of the Earth."[118]

The page of "Acknowledgments" in the front of the Brady School pamphlet ends with this sentence: "We wish to express our appreciation to the Superintendent and members of his staff who have reviewed this booklet and approved its use in the Detroit public schools."[119]

2. *Assembly programs designed to provide short inspirational periods, usually at the beginning of the day.* The purpose here too is the religious development of the pupils, but the plan is usually far less elaborate than the one in the Brady School. Generally, there is no organized, consistent attempt throughout the school to practice the virtues emphasized in the program. "Morning Meditations" in the Warren G. Harding Senior High School, Warren, Ohio, is an example of this type.

The teacher of speech in that school reports that until a few years ago the homeroom devotionals were a chore unpleasant to the teachers and pupils alike. They consisted of a Bible passage read aloud by an unwilling youngster, usually a girl, followed by the Lord's Prayer repeated in concert "while the teacher, with head bowed, kept one eye cocked on pupils to discourage their attempts to complete geometry assignments."[120] Then one teacher timidly suggested to the principal that one devotional program be carefully prepared each day for the whole school and broadcast over the public address system to the 1800 students. The proposal was tried, and everyone liked it. The plan is still in operation, and there is always a waiting list of students eager to take part. A typical program is described as follows:

After 30 seconds of organ music, the reader for the day begins with a few Bible verses, selected because they strike the keynote of a message to be illustrated. The scripture is interpreted by means of a story chosen for its appeal to high school listeners. Then comes a simply worded prayer. A few measures of the recording close the devotional.[121]

3. *Religious forum with attendance optional.* In the Junior-Senior High School of Marshall, Missouri, several forum groups are organized each year around religious topics selected by the students. Some of the most popular subjects are: How does prayer work? What should I think about God? Can religion help preserve the peace? What should church membership mean to me? Is there a conflict between science and religion? The speakers are religious leaders of the various faiths represented in the school. The students prefer out-of-town leaders because they think it is easier to ask strangers those questions which they most want to ask. Although attendance is optional, more than four-fifths of the students participate.[122]

4. *Assembly programs which emphasize religious attitudes on special subjects.* For example, in River Forest, Illinois, the junior high school pupils in a "released-time" class in religious education planned and conducted several assembly

programs in the public school on the subject of racial equality.[123] Programs of this kind might be used to analyze and call attention to a variety of contemporary problems.

5. *Assembly programs to celebrate special days.* Many public schools include religious materials in special programs to celebrate Armistice Day, Thanksgiving, Christmas, Memorial Day, and the birthdays of great Americans. Helpful suggestions on how to make clear the religious significance of several of the holidays are in Manwell and Fahs' *Consider the Children—How They Grow.*[124]

6. *The music assembly.* Some schools have excellent assembly programs consisting entirely of singing and listening to good music. Many of them include religious music.

RELIGION IN EDUCATIONAL AND VOCATIONAL GUIDANCE

Most of the conditions essential to the integration of religion into the guidance program will already have been met when the study of religion in the various subjects of the school curriculum has become the normal practice. That is, as the children and youth begin to understand better the significance of religion in history and its meaning and goals today, its influence on the guidance program will follow as a matter of course. Evidence that this point has been reached will appear not so much in changes in the organizational plan for guidance as in new emphases in what is already being done. Several examples will show what some of these new emphases are likely to be.

1. *A search for the sources of contentment in life.* Children cannot study and discuss the kinds of problems suggested throughout this chapter without frequently finding occasions to inquire, What does it take to make life worth living? An

attempt to answer this question may become a special project in some aspect of group guidance or it may be considered incidentally whenever it seems relevant to other problems. Groups interested in this subject may want to consider such steps as the following:

a. Interview representatives of various occupations to find out if they would choose the same vocation again if the opportunity for a new decision were possible. Analyze their reasons.

b. Study one of the many surveys which have been made to discover the actual as contrasted with the preferred occupations of employed youth. Try to decide why so many of them are unhappy in their work. Is Super right when he suggests that parents who insist that their children climb high on the social ladder often contribute to this unhappiness?[125]

c. Try to answer this question: Are there some kinds of vocations which should be avoided by persons seeking genuine contentment?

d. Read and discuss as a group one or more such books as Fosdick's *On Being a Real Person*[126] or Liebman's *Peace of Mind*.[127]

e. Discuss and evaluate ideas on contentment as suggested by current motion pictures. The Protestant Film Commission's picture *Beyond Our Own* also would serve this purpose.

2. Provision for supplying information on religious vocations. This information will be factual, but often challenging to youth. In many schools it will start with class assignments on the world of work including the religious vocations. But for some students such a beginning may well lead to interviews with outstanding religious leaders, to participation in carefully selected religious programs, and to reading the

biographies of persons like Wesley, Gandhi, Kagawa, and Schweitzer.

3. *Attention to religion in the testing program.* This means that those in charge of testing will seek constantly to discover among youth special interest in and aptitude for religious leadership as well as interests and aptitudes of other kinds.

4. *Inclusion of religion in counseling.* In schools large enough to have counseling teams, a competent religious counselor will serve along with psychiatrists, psychologists, social workers, and other specialists. In schools where this arrangement is not possible, the guidance staff may have a referral agreement with one or more clergymen qualified to work with individuals or groups in need of the kinds of help which religious leadership can most readily give. Also, when the counseling centers upon the choice of life's work, the religious vocations will be given their fair share of attention.

5. *Guidance in preparation for specialized training.* As the school discovers young people who are seriously considering religious vocations, it will assist them to contact religious leaders well qualified to guide them in making definite plans. This guidance should include detailed conferences with religious leaders, the choice of a school for professional training, and attention to such problems as scholarships, finance, and perhaps the tentative selection of an area of specialization.

RELIGIOUS MATERIALS IN THE LIBRARY

The role of the library in experimentation with a study of religion in the public schools is very difficult because of the scarcity of good materials. Those responsible for making pur-

chases may want to select some of the books and other helps
referred to in this chapter. However, in every case these
materials should be examined first by the librarians, teachers,
and other educational leaders upon whom their successful
use will depend. It is recommended that the librarians be
included in all the preliminary study and discussion leading
up to the beginning of the experiment. Otherwise, requests
for their help as the experimentation gets under way cannot
possibly bring satisfactory library service.

The kinds of religious materials selected for the library
should include books, pamphlets, clippings, reproductions of
great paintings, films and film strips, and records and transcriptions. In addition to the religious subject matter provided for integration into the various parts of the school
curriculum, it is important that libraries keep complete sets
of pamphlets describing the different kinds of religious vocations. Also, there should be up-to-date files of college and
seminary catalogues for use in vocational guidance and for
senior high school students to examine as they wish.

As all librarians know,

Books and materials should be of such quality that they will
stimulate and inspire intellectual, cultural, social, and moral
development; and they should be selected with the maturity and
capacity of the group to be served as a guiding principle.[128]

In selecting religious materials for use in the public schools
it is suggested that recommendations be sought from the
official representatives of all the denominations in the community and also from competent persons not affiliated with
any religious body.

Finally, of course, certain basic aids to make libraries functional should be available. For example, to increase the use-
fulness of the magazine collection the *Reader's Guide to*

Periodical Literature is a necessity. Guidance in the area of audio-visual aids is provided by such books as Dale's *Audio-Visual Methods in Teaching*[129] and Strauss and Kidd's *Look, Listen, and Learn.*[130] Ultimately, however, much of the responsibility for the effective use of the materials must rest with the librarians who alone have it within their power to make the library a challenging and pleasant place in which to work.

3 Matters of Policy

A major source of difficulty likely to characterize serious attempts at experimentation with an objective study of religion in public education grows out of the fact that even the most competent and sincere leaders will sometimes disagree on matters of basic policy. For this reason, representative groups within the community should carefully study each proposal and its implications before trying to put it into operation. Suggestions as to how this preliminary study and discussion might proceed will be given in Chapter 5. The purpose here is to identify some of the main issues involved and to assist leaders to see clearly the kinds of decisions that will have to be made in each local community desiring to experiment in accordance with this plan. These aims will be considered under three headings, as follows:

1. *Criteria for weighing matters of policy.* The list of principles in this section is suggested as a measuring rod for judging points to be examined later in this chapter.

2. *Questions considered elsewhere.* Some essential questions of policy have been considered incidentally as they have appeared in earlier chapters while others belong naturally to later parts of this report. They are mentioned here only to emphasize their importance in this setting.

3. *Major controversial issues.* Attention is given here to five such matters by examining each of them in the light of the criteria suggested for that purpose.

CRITERIA FOR WEIGHING MATTERS OF POLICY

This list of criteria consists of statements of six general principles. It is assumed that most educational and religious leaders in America will find them acceptable. However, if changes in these principles are considered necessary by leaders who are planning experiments, it is important that such changes be clearly understood by all concerned before proceeding further.

1. Both federal and state regulations on this subject should be strictly obeyed. For example, it is clear that many of the suggestions in Chapter 2 cannot be followed legally in states which prohibit reading the Bible in public schools. To attempt to circumvent such a law is obviously unwise. Interested leaders in these states should consider only innovations which are clearly within the letter and spirit of the law.

2. The principle of the separation of church and state should be carefully observed. As stated earlier, the separation of church and state means "that the church and state are mutually free. It means separation of control, so that neither the church nor the state will attempt to control the other."[1] For representatives of any religious denomination or sect to attempt either directly or indirectly to exercise undue influence upon publicly supported schools is a violation of this basic principle. Boards of education should avoid any action which might place one or more religious groups in positions of special privilege.

3. The generally accepted policy on the relation of religion to public education in the United States allows considerable freedom for an objective study of religion but opposes sectarian indoctrination in every form. The American Council's Committee on Religion and Education carefully uses the phrase "the study of religion" in contrast to " teaching re-

ligion" because to many Americans the latter expression suggests a purpose of indoctrination.[2] In the opinion of this committee, public schools are clearly within their rights when they ask children to study religion objectively and even when they urge the young to take some stand on religious matters. The committee writes: "To be educated does not mean to have been taught what to think, but it does mean to have learned what to think *about* and to have acquired definite convictions with respect to values."[3]

However, some Americans who are favorable to the basic proposals in this project feel that it is best for public schools to leave entirely to the religious bodies the responsibility for urging children and youth to take a stand on religious questions. If this possible objection to the committee's report is resolved by agreeing that the schools will help children to understand the facts and implications of religious teachings but will not aim at any kind of commitment, it would seem that this general principle should be acceptable to everyone. Certainly all teachers who value academic freedom would resent regulations designed to prevent an objective study of religion in the public schools if interpreted in this way. The acceptance of any plan to eliminate this kind of attention to religious subject matter would seem to endanger the freedom of the schools in other areas too.

4. The principle of complete freedom of religion should be preserved. This principle includes the right of every person to accept any religion that he chooses or to reject all religion, in either case with impunity. It would not seem to be a violation of religious liberty to ask all children to study objectively the various forms of religion, but to insist that they engage in religious exercises against their will would be a violation of this principle. The latter requirement would in effect be forcing the young to pass from a study of the

meaning of religion to participation in the practice of religion. The public school teacher who insists, for example, that all children participate in singing hymns as an experience of worship cannot properly defend his action. Similarly, the secularist teacher in a tax-supported institution violates the principle of religious liberty if he "teaches" his philosophy "which negates the religious beliefs of millions of Americans.[4] The error in both instances is the same: each attempts to by-pass with his pupils an objective study of the many forms of religion and to use instead an approach which may correctly be called indoctrination.

5. Leaders in experimentation should be sensitive to the felt needs and personal attitudes of all groups affected. The two following recommendations in this connection may be helpful:

a. The initial study and discussion should center around concrete problems in the minds of all parents. For example, what more can the school do to help children grow into decent adults in this difficult world? It is best to build confidence by demonstrating what the school can do toward solving some specific problems before going too deeply into the more controversial areas suggested for experimentation.

b. It is generally unwise to publicize widely the plans for special projects. Often the result of too much publicity is the appearance of opposition which otherwise would not have been felt.

Some leaders have suggested that in many communities an objective study of religion in the public schools will be more likely to succeed if the teachers are cautioned to avoid traditional religious phraseology. They recognize, of course, that it is not always possible to observe this principle literally.

6. Specific plans for the settlement of controversial matters should be agreed to by the leaders before the experimenta-

tion begins. This does not require a procedure by which complete harmony can be assured but rather a recognition of the fact that in some areas perfect agreement may not be possible. For example, if some groups within a given community are unwilling to have the public schools analyze and criticize their beliefs, perhaps these groups could agree to permit an official spokesman for each to interpret his group to the children who in turn would be free to ask him questions. This would provide some attention to the various points of view even though with less freedom than most educators might wish. In considering what policy should be followed when fundamental differences of opinion arise, local leaders might find it helpful to examine the four following possibilities:

a. Omit from the curriculum every topic which even the smallest minority objects to including. This is what has happened during the last century in much of America with the unsatisfactory results which this report seeks to help correct.

b. Arrange for public school children to be exposed to written and spoken interpretations of the different points of view as presented by the official leaders of each group, but discourage free investigation and discussion in the classes.

c. Provide for children to study and discuss the various points of view under the guidance of well-trained public school teachers who are instructed to emphasize the best in all religions. The independent Shady Side Academy of Pittsburgh follows a plan comparable to this. The following statement in the school's brochure explains this position:

We believe that theological problems are important, and should be dealt with head-on in the life of the Academy. . . . Our Students come from all major denominations and groups. . . . We believe that our boys should try to live up to the best their own faith has to offer. To that end, we attempt to make plain . . . what the various religious groups stand for. We do not try to minimize sincere differences of opinion. We try to inculcate an understanding of what each group believes, to enlighten the members of each, and to make clear what other groups affirm. Only in this way can our unity in diversity be maintained.[5]

d. Give to public school teachers and their pupils complete freedom to study objectively, analyze, and criticize the history, achievements, and emphases of all religious groups. The aim would be to help each young person to think his own way through the central problems of religion, thereby providing him with an intellectual basis for action.

QUESTIONS CONSIDERED ELSEWHERE

Six main questions of policy belong in this classification. The first two were discussed in Chapter 1, the third is clearly implied by the whole plan outlined in Chapter 2, and the fourth, fifth, and sixth will be dealt with later in this report. As stated above, they are mentioned at this point only to emphasize their importance in this setting.

1. Experimentation as suggested in this report will probably be most welcome in religiously homogeneous communities, but in such communities the danger is greatest that the policy of studying religion objectively will not be adhered to. Opportunities for real pioneering in this area are greatest in places characterized by wide diversity of religious faiths. Those who favor indoctrination in the religious beliefs held by the people in homogeneous communities have in mind goals which are not acceptable to the American Council's Committee on Religion and Education.

2. All public schools should follow the lead of the best

ones in emphasizing moral and spiritual values, but this is not enough. After indicating its willingness to defend schools sometimes attacked for giving attention to such values the committee continues,

But to assume that spiritual values embody the full, valid content of religion is quite another matter. The words "spiritual" and "moral" denote the value-structure of life. Religion seeks personal identification with some ultimate source of values. It involves faith in the permanent validity and durability of these values. Religion has always supplied moral sanctions for men's actions. No person is fully educated who has not gained a knowledge of the faiths men live by. And unless the schools are content to leave one of the major areas of life unexplored, the specifically religious beliefs and aspirations of human beings must have attention.[6]

3. Textbooks used in the public schools generally omit religious subject matter, but this does not prevent giving attention to religion in the classrooms. All good teachers know that effective education requires the constant use of many kinds of materials besides textbooks, as reference on special subjects, encyclopedias, biographies, historical novels, speeches, magazines, maps, charts, excursions, radio programs, phonograph records and transcriptions, films and film strips, and other helps. It is true that new religious materials are needed if religion is to be studied extensively in public schools, but such materials will appear rapidly if the demand for them increases. In the meantime, alert teachers can make an excellent beginning with the books and related aids already available.

4. A clear policy on the selection and training of teachers should be established before actual experimentation begins. Suggestions on this problem will be presented in Chapter 4.

5. As experimentation in each community proceeds, the

desirability of evaluating the results will become apparent. Some possible methods will be considered in Chapter 6.

6. Experience in seeking the best ways to integrate religious subject matter into the public school curriculum will undoubtedly emphasize the fact that what the school can achieve alone is unlikely to be very significant. Only if the churches and synagogues, homes, and other community agencies also perform their duties better is it reasonable to expect satisfactory results. In Chapter 6 attention will be given to the possibility of community-wide planning to coordinate and improve the services of all these agencies.

MAJOR CONTROVERSIAL ISSUES

This section is a survey of five of the major matters of policy which must inevitably appear wherever public schools undertake experimentation with an objective study of religion. It is doubtful if there is any single right position with respect to any of these five issues. It is recommended that leaders of experiments study the basic analyses as presented here and then try to find solutions best suited to the peculiar needs of the community concerned. During this process of analysis the six criteria for weighing matters of policy as described above should be used as bases of judgment.

1. The first of these major controversial issues concerns the place of a functional approach in the study of religion in public schools. Early in Chapter 2 a statement was made to the effect that the use of a functional approach in the proposed experimentation might lead to indoctrination. This statement may require an explanation.

Generally, when one thinks of a functional approach to any kind of education he means that the process includes the immediate use of what is learned. Thus, newly acquired knowledge becomes immediately functional. Most leading educators consider such an approach to be educationally sound. They insist, for example, that it is not enough to study about how governments operate. While they agree that teachers can force children to memorize facts, they contend that these facts will not take on much real meaning until they are used. Mort and Vincent write:

This means that the best way to train for a part is to play a part. That is why the "school of experience" is such a good teacher. When schools must train pupils to play parts in a real world, the school is most successful which is as real and as like the world at its best as is possible—a school where pupils, in the presence of wise counselors, face and solve real problems of living as preparation for doing just that in later life.[7]

This seems like sound theory, and many of our schools are striving earnestly to reach such an ideal. However, the experiences in some communities indicate that sincere attempts to use schools as laboratories for practice in facing vital problems in life are not always acceptable to the people. For example, many American parents are willing to have their children study and discuss the ideal of racial equality but oppose school projects in which their children are expected to associate with the young of other races on an equal basis. Or, boards of education and school administrators and teachers may take it as a matter of course that children study and discuss in the classroom the arguments for and against organized labor, but may be hesitant to sanction plans among the high school students to organize themselves to improve the school.

Such examples indicate that adults are usually willing for children to study and discuss controversial subjects in the classroom, but when schools encourage pupils to engage in actual practice in doing things which some groups in the community disapprove, objections appear. And the more controversial the issue, the more violent the opposition will be. If this conclusion is correct, it seems fair to assume that many people would be willing to accept a purely objective study of religion in the public schools while objecting to a school policy requiring participation in religious exercises. Such persons would argue that to study religion to gain a knowledge of its origins, history, goals, and methods may not be objectionable, but to insist that children engage in religious practices of any kind is intolerable. The latter policy, they would contend, would mean that the school accepts the religious point of view as the right one and attempts to force all children into that pattern. This would be a kind of indoctrination and clearly a violation of the principle of religious liberty.

Therefore, while it may not be possible to separate entirely the knowledge of religion from the practice of religion, it seems clear that in the public schools the only emphasis possible is on the knowledge aspect. Many people are of the opinion that such knowledge is inevitably functional even though this may not be the main purpose for which it has been acquired. Those who urge public schools to experiment with an objective study of religion say that such a program would have religious literacy as its goal. That is, it would supply the young with a knowledge of religion which, they believe, would serve as an intellectual basis for appraising and making meaningful their participation in the religious programs provided for them by their churches and synagogues. This would mean that the suggested innovation in the public school program would ultimately be functional even though this effect would be a by-product and not the immediate goal.

On the other hand, as some educators interpret the functional approach to teaching, the actual practice of the principles learned is not a necessary part. Such persons would insist, however, that the schools should insure a clear understanding of basic principles and their implications by requiring the study and discussion of what they would mean in actual practice. If functional teaching is interpreted in this way, it would be a legitimate and necessary part of the plan suggested here.

Perhaps the central idea for local leaders to remember in this discussion is that whenever the public schools go beyond a purely objective study of religion and require children actually to engage in any kind of religious exercises, the effect may be the denial of someone's freedom of religion. It is suggested, however, that teachers would not violate this principle by encouraging pupils to face and discuss objectively real moral issues as they arise naturally in the classroom in connection with their study of religion.

2. The second major controversial issue is closely related to the first. It concerns religious practices which already exist in many public schools in this country—practices which are generally accepted in communities because they are in accordance with the religious beliefs of a majority of the people. Religious leaders and educators who are serious in their desire to provide genuine religious liberty for all should ask themselves if these practices are actually satisfactory to the secularists and the religious minorities represented in the schools. Typical of such practices are three which require special emphasis.

a. Worship exercises in assembly programs. The Brady School Plan in Detroit and the "morning meditations" in the Warren G. Harding Senior High School, Warren, Ohio, both of which were described in Chapter 2, are examples. The Los Angeles schools employ similar practices when they set out specifically to develop in children a "faith in God."[8] Such practices are common in many states, though perhaps they are carried on more thoughtfully and with greater effectiveness in the cities named here than in most places. While respecting the leaders in these schools for trying to do well what they consider to be legitimate practices, many people would question the soundness of such goals in the public schools.

b. Religious celebrations of special days, as Thanksgiving, Christmas, Easter, and the Jewish Hanukkah. During the 1947 Christmas season feelings ran high for several days in Brooklyn, New York, and in San Francisco, California, over the question of singing Christmas carols in the public schools. Those who opposed the practice argued that it is a violation of religious liberty to expect children of Jewish and other non-Christian parents to participate in celebrations which are meaningful only to Christians.

c. Bible reading. The reading of the Bible in public schools has often been opposed by Jews and Roman Catholics "on the ground that the Bible used was a Protestant Bible and therefore sectarian in their eyes."[9]

There are no simple solutions to the problems raised by these practices in typical public schools in our country, but they are problems which cannot be ignored. It may be that in some communities the people will prefer to continue these religious practices in spite of the objections just mentioned. If such a policy is adopted, it is important that the leaders act with full understanding of the implications of the step they are taking. Furthermore, it is suggested that they explain these implications to all the people and indicate their willingness to make alterations in the plan if requested to do so by individuals or groups. Leaders who prefer to make changes before there has been any further opportunity for criticisms to develop may find the following suggestions helpful:

a. Simple exercises of worship in assembly programs might be justified on the grounds that certain forms of worship— for example, saying the Lord's Prayer or the Twenty-third Psalm—are a part of our culture and that persons unaccustomed to such common experiences are not properly educated.

b. Worship in general assembly programs and in the celebration of special days might be continued but with definite arrangements to excuse children at the request of their parents. If worship periods were placed at the beginning or the end of the school day, it would not be difficult to plan for non-participation of some pupils. Probably the number of requests for these excuses would be very small in most American communities, particularly if school authorities were careful to plan devotional exercises which are nonsectarian in the sense that they actually transcend the emphases peculiar to individual sects. For example, it is unlikely that many parents would object to having their children participate reverently in reading and discussing the Psalm beginning with the sentence, "The heavens declare the glory of God, and the firmament showeth his handiwork."[10] Indeed, it seems to many people that the wise choice of the scriptural passages to be read in the public schools might eliminate the necessity for the "reading-without-comment" regulations in several states. It should be clearly understood, of course, that any provision to excuse children from services of worship would not apply to the regular classes in which only a purely objective study of religion would occur.

c. Non-Christian groups in some communities might be willing to participate in such activities as singing Christmas carols even though the practice has no religious significance for them, as a means of furthering good will or with the purpose of understanding their neighbors or simply for the enjoyment of group singing. If it is proper to ask children of all races to study and to sing Negro spirituals as a method of understanding and appreciating the Negro race, it would seem that non-Christian parents might be glad for their children to join in singing Christmas carols for a similar reason. Some Jews have clearly expressed themselves as feeling that the Christmas carols issue is not of sufficient importance to justify the intergroup tensions which have sometimes developed. One Jewish leader in Brooklyn, New York, for example, speaking for himself only, says:

I cannot see any particular evil for Jewish children to join with non-Jewish children in celebrating a festival occasion with a long historic background that is widely observed and recognized, even though it may concern a religious symbol.[11]

In a similar manner and for the same reasons it is suggested that children of Christian and other non-Jewish homes should gladly join Jewish children in the celebration of such important holidays and festivals as the Hanukkah.

d. A possible solution to the problem growing out of opposition to the use of a Protestant Bible is suggested by the president of the Ogontz Junior College in Pennsylvania. She writes: "Each girl has her own Bible including the Catholic girls who have the Vulgate or Douay version in their hands" as the classroom discussion centers around selected passages.[12] A second possibility is not to read the Bible at all, but to use books of Bible stories.

3. Another controversial issue which should be squarely

faced by religious and educational leaders before attempting
the kind of experimentation suggested in this report concerns
the critical examination of the beliefs and practices of the
various sects. Both religious leaders and educators are among
those who feel that the public schools should have complete
freedom in this respect. One religious leader writes:

If institutionalized religion is outmoded, the quickest way to
discard it would be to include in the school a discussion of its
beliefs and practices, so that they might be subjected to the
critique of reason and the searchlight of historical and scientific
truth. If theology is invalid, then it would be a great service to
the total community if all the people could be taught the truth,
as well as the reasons for its invalidation. . . .

Our failure to subject our religious beliefs and practices to
open criticism and examination has encouraged the cults of
snake-handlers, fanatics, and all sorts of reactionaries, so that the
religiously illiterate fall easy prey to pseudo-religious schemers.
Thus, the least adequate and least intelligent forms of religion
often flourish, and the total program of institutionalized religion
at its best is less effective than it might otherwise be, for it is in
a degree freed from the refining fires of objective community
criticism.[13]

A group of educators expresses this opinion:

Whenever and wherever the leaders and adherents of the
various churches agree that the creeds and rival claims and
practices of religion can be studied by the ordinary empirical
procedures characteristic of the other work of the public school,
little difficulty will be experienced in making these aspects of
religion also a part of the program of public education.[14]

In examining the practicability of these suggestions for
use in American communities, local leaders will also want to
consider the other possibilities stated in the last of the six

criteria for weighing matters of policy as described on pages 72-74. It is probable that one or more religious groups in most communities would be unhappy if the public schools were immediately allowed complete freedom in this area. And many Americans, including large numbers of the teachers themselves, are of the opinion that public school teachers on the whole are almost totally unprepared at this time to assume any such responsibilities even if the religious groups did not object.

It seems obvious that no outsider can answer this question for any community. If local leaders are unable to agree on a plan which is reasonably satisfactory to all concerned, it is probably best to stop at this point any further consideration of the proposed experimentation in the public schools. However, communities which believe that the objectives sought are worth some real sacrifices by the various groups may want to consider a plan calling for gradually allowing the schools more power in the area of objective study and criticism of all sects as the teachers responsible prove themselves capable. The following is suggestive of a type of plan which might be acceptable to all groups in some places:

a. First year: Invite priests, ministers, rabbis, and secularists to present their basic beliefs to the children who are old enough to understand the main elements in each point of view. Each such spokesman should suggest supplementary readings for further study in the school. It is essential, of course, that the leaders chosen to speak for their people be persons who understand the public school goals in the study of religion and who are recognized throughout the community for their fairness in dealing with groups whose beliefs differ from their own.

b. Second year: Repeat the procedure of the first year,

allowing more time and more freedom in the school for study and discussion of the differences as well as the likenesses.

c. Third year: Repeat the procedures of the first two years, but allow complete freedom to study, compare, criticize, and evaluate the beliefs and practices of all groups.

Such a plan would allow several years for the public school teachers to prepare themselves more adequately to guide children and youth wisely in this difficult undertaking. Also, it would provide opportunities for the board of education, school administration, and the educational and religious leaders in the experiment to observe the results and to revise their plans as suggested by experience.

4. There is an important issue, too, about the interpretation of the Bible. The local leaders in each community desiring to experiment with an objective study of religion in public education will have to answer this question: What attitude should teachers in the public school assume if individuals or groups represented in the community insist that the Bible be "taught" as the revealed word of God instead of being "studied" as one of the great religious classics?

It is unrealistic to assume that this problem will not arise. In his evaluation of the 1947 report of the American Council's Committee on Religion and Education, Smith writes:

If the Bible is to become a part of the content of courses in literature, surely it must be studied as thoroughly and with as much intellectual respect as is paid to a Dickens novel or a Shakespearean drama. This means that the historical facts about the origin of the scriptures and their subsequent career would be studied; it means that the various interpretations of biblical passages would be examined and an effort made to evaluate them; it means that biblical characters would be analyzed.[15]

In Smith's opinion such a study is certain to lead to bitter conflicts in typical communities in America.

In Moehlman's famous chapter on "Can the Bible Return to the Classroom?" he predicts that any board of education unwise enough to undertake experimentation involving this attempt would probably

appoint Miss Mary Prudent as best fitted by background, interest, and personality to make the classes in religion a great success.

To enable her to prepare more effectively, the Board would select a number of general books on the Bible, source books, dictionaries, translations, cross-reference Bibles, commentaries, stories of the Bible, concordances, and "Bible helps." The reference list would represent all shades of opinion so that the needs of all the children might be met. *Over two hundred and fifty different religious groups in the country require over two hundred and fifty different kinds of handling.* Of course neither the Board nor Miss Prudent would fully understand what would happen in the classroom when orthodoxy met heresy; sect, denomination; cult, fundamentalism; scientist's son, minister's daughter; communist, fascist; atheist, believer; neutral, Nazi; pacifist, marine. "Just for today" is a good motto for the public school teacher of the Bible.[16]

Those who think that this is an exaggerated description of the dangers inherent in the proposal cite such statements as those by Bower and Morrison as quoted on page 19 above and point out the wide variety of existing practices, including Bible-reading in public schools required by law in many states, as presented in the NEA Research Bulletin entitled *The State and Sectarian Education.*[17]

It is of course impossible to predict with certainty what actually would happen in any given community in which the Bible was studied consistently in the public schools by all the methods suggested in this report. In Chapter 2 the five following plans for using the Bible in literature classes were discussed:

a. Incidental study of the Bible as background for the appreciation of English literature and the English language. For example, such commonly used expressions as "the handwriting on the wall" become more meaningful if one knows their Biblical origin.

b. Correlation of the Bible with literature, as the story of the Good Samaritan (Luke 10:30-36) with Hunt's poem "Abou Ben Adhem."

c. Reading Bible stories.

d. Emphasis on great passages in the Bible.

e. Survey courses on the Bible.

Many people believe that the first four of these five methods could be used in literature classes in most communities with very little danger of conflict, provided all the people participated in formulating the plan in the first place. The fifth method would not be tried except in an occasional senior high school in which one or more teachers highly trained in religion were available. If children asked the public school teacher whether the Bible is infallible, he might reply that religious leaders do not agree on this question but that all do agree that the Bible is a great book that every educated person should know, adding that only scholars who have specialized in Bible study for years are qualified to discuss the deeper meanings of the scriptures. It would seem that he might then explain his own opinion about the question asked and arrange for the class to read or hear other points of view. Obviously a teacher who is not thoroughly trained in religion should freely admit this fact and state that he is not prepared to answer the profound religious questions about which religious leaders themselves often disagree.

5. Finally, in some communities the official leaders of some of the religious faiths may state frankly that they consider any plan for an objective study of religion in the schools

to be quite impractical. Some may even say that if required to choose between this method and no religious education at all they would unhesitatingly choose the latter. In defense of such an attitude, they would probably argue that religion cannot be understood by study and discussion but must be accepted by faith alone. They would insist, perhaps, that what is needed is: first, belief and commitment; second, church membership; and finally, growth in religious living within the church or synagogue. None of these phases in their opinion would be advanced by the objective study suggested in this project.

If an attitude comparable to this exists among the religious leaders, it is important to discover and face it realistically before initiating an experiment in the schools. It is the opinion of the Committee on Religion and Education that an objective study of religion in the public schools is sound both educationally and religiously. The committee does not claim that such a program would provide all the essentials of either religious learning or living, but it sees the plan as a means of developing through the schools a solid foundation upon which the homes, churches, and synagogues could build. If the responsible religious leaders in the community are unable to accept such a proposal as sound, it is obvious that school officials would be unwise to insist upon undertaking the experiment in the face of such opposition.

4 Selecting and Training Teachers

Much of the responsibility for the success or failure of experiments growing out of these proposals must inevitably rest upon the teachers. Freehof argues that only unsatisfactory results are possible because he believes that teachers cannot really be objective in religious matters. In his opinion, "no comment on the Protestant church by Catholic teachers or on the Catholic church by Protestant teachers, or on Judaism by Christian teachers, or on Christianity by Jewish teachers, can fail to be inadequate and unintentionally deprecatory or unjust."[1]

Although the American Council's Committee on Religion and Education does not accept this blanket statement, it does recognize the importance of the problem, expressing its attitude in these words:

Two dangers loom large in the process: first, the danger inherent in the fact that there are large numbers of teachers who are not adequately informed in matters of religion and who lack interest in the study of religion; and second, the danger arising from the fact that teachers with deep religious convictions are tempted to teach religion along sectarian lines. These dangers are not unsurmountable and do not represent vulnerabilities which cannot be overcome by good teacher education.[2]

The suggestions in this chapter are based upon two assumptions: first, that the committee is right in believing that public school teachers can be trained to deal with religion objectively in the classroom; and second, that the religious groups represented in communities desiring to experiment will not oppose an objective study of religion in the public schools under the direction of lay teachers.

The preparation of teachers, like all other phases of the proposal, requires experimentation which should continue over a period of years. Progress is certain to be slow, particularly until teacher training institutions assume a major role in the task. It is clear that this will not occur until local communities begin to request teachers trained in religion as well as in other aspects of the culture. At the present time, therefore, it seems likely that communities desiring to undertake experimentation will have to take the initiative in providing basic training for the teachers. The purpose of this chapter is to offer some guidance on this subject to local leaders.

SPECIAL ATTITUDES AND ABILITIES DESIRABLE IN TEACHERS
WHO LEAD

Most of the qualities suggested in this section as desirable in teachers assuming leadership in the proposed program are qualities characteristic of all good teachers. However, they are probably more necessary here than in many other kinds of teaching and learning situations because serious deficiencies in this instance might produce wounds particularly difficult to heal. The qualifications considered to be the most essential are of six kinds:

1. *Intellectual competence.* Hook uses this phrase to mean a "capacity for analysis," which is "something different from mere possession of the dry-bones and heaps of knowledge."[3] It includes adequate information about the method of ar-

riving at facts as well as knowledge of what the facts are, and it requires the ability to explain this method to others in language which they can understand. Teachers recommended for leadership in this program must be well oriented in several fields of knowledge besides their specialty and religion, and must strive constantly to make this broad background functional in their teaching. Also, they must know and take seriously the implications of the major discoveries in the field of educational psychology. Mort considers the five following principles to be the nucleus of these discoveries most relevant to educational practices today:

a. The theory of formal discipline is no longer acceptable. "There is no simple generally applicable curriculum that prepares for life by training the mind."[4]

b. Individuals "differ in all sorts of ways," and it is the responsibility of the school to provide a wide variety of experiences so that each may get the kinds of help which he needs.[5]

c. Learning is most meaningful when it is promptly put to use in everyday life situations.[6]

d. Learning must start where the pupil is.[7]

e. Interest indicates where the learner is ready to develop.[8]

Chapter 5 in Williams' *The New Education and Religion*[9] is a helpful discussion of effective methods of teaching with emphasis on religious subject matter.

2. *Participation in community life.* All good teachers know the importance of establishing "a condition of mutual trust, understanding, and sympathy, not only with the community leaders and representatives, but with all the people."[10] They know that respect for their worth grows as they demonstrate a sincere interest in many good causes by cooperating in the activities of various community clubs, societies, and organizations. If they consistently follow democratic procedures in

these activities, the people will know that they do not have undemocratic motives in their more purely educational duties in the schoolroom. Teachers responsible for leadership in studying religion objectively in the public schools should include among their close personal friends representatives of the three major faiths, especially one or more priests, ministers, and rabbis.

3. *Creativity in teaching.* Truth-finding seems to be a native desire in all of us. An objective study of religion offers many opportunities to preserve and strengthen this quality in children and youth, but only creative teachers are likely to meet this challenge successfully. Such teachers are like other creative adults whom Mearns describes as "those who come daily to original judgment, who respect their own sense of what is good and true and beautiful, who are unafraid of the imputation either of ignorance or of low caste but only of the accusation of untruthfulness."[11]

Teachers who are themselves creative can profit from Mearns' advice as to adult behavior likely to encourage the development of creativity in others. After experimenting with children from three to eight years of age for several summers he wrote:

After much trial and error I found eventually the procedures which opened the welcoming door into the secret individual life. They were mainly: to move and speak with exaggerated slowness; to listen without comment; to ask no questions at all until I had learned to inquire without implying accusation of sin; then to remove every vibration of superiority from eyes, voice tones and even posture; and finally to receive without intrusion of instruction and with surely never a show of surprise. . . . With necessary changes, of course, these procedures turn out to be the principles of opening right communications with any age group.[12]

4. *Emotional security.* Except for an occasional misfit employed to an educational staff through someone's error, the main responsibility for providing teachers who possess emotional security rests with the board of education. Teachers who are made to feel inferior by school administrators, whose salaries are insufficient to allow a satisfactory standard of living, or who are constantly harassed by unfair demands from the public, cannot be expected to succeed as leaders in the program proposed in this report. Communities which are serious in their desire to experiment with this or other projects in educational pioneering should begin by insisting upon the adoption of school board policies guaranteeing to teachers:

a. Salaries high enough to give their profession a first-class status among other professions in the community.

b. Permanent tenure, following a probationary period.

c. Reasonable freedom from public meddling into their private lives.

d. Freedom from discrimination because of race, creed, political beliefs, or marital status.

e. A fair share in the formulation of school policy.

f. A degree of academic freedom essential to the encouragement of honest study and discussion of controversial issues in the classroom. The American Council's Committee on Religion and Education makes it clear that such freedom does not imply the right of teachers to practice sectarian indoctrination in matters of religion.[13]

5. *Genuine respect for sincerely religious members of all faiths.* This qualification can be expected to eliminate from leadership the crusader whose ambition is to make the classroom a place to convert children to a particular belief. As emphasized throughout this report, influencing the young to accept a personal religion is not an objective of this plan.

Most of the regular lay teachers in the public schools all over America should be satisfactory leaders in this program provided they first receive a fair amount of special training in preparation for the task. Naturally, many such teachers would be members of various religious bodies—Roman Catholic, Protestant, and Jewish—and some of them would be persons who accept no religious faith. Concerning this latter group Sutton writes:

> Teachers not holding religious convictions could be expected to state a religious interpretation as to views which certain others sincerely hold, and do so with the same tolerance that the true teacher manifests toward differing opinions in any field.[14]

6. *Mature attitudes toward pupils.* In typical classes in the public schools several religious points of view can be expected. Some pupils may be very spirited in their denial of the claims of certain religious groups or may even argue that all religion is meaningless or false. Other children may find it difficult to face criticisms of beliefs which they have been taught to accept. Teachers should be prepared to soften blows for those who need support and to balance radical or destructive statements with the saner and more constructive opinions of others. The aim should be to encourage real thinking, at the same time helping children and youth to learn to discuss controversial issues honestly without developing personal feelings of bitterness toward those who disagree with them.

MOTIVATION OF PUBLIC SCHOOL TEACHERS TO ASSUME LEADERSHIP

Many public school teachers hesitate to align themselves with individuals or groups undertaking projects of a religious nature because they feel unable to approve certain emphases which they associate with their own earlier contacts with religious programs. To many of them religion suggests various kinds of mysticism which they do not understand and calls to mind certain people whom they find it difficult to admire.

Perhaps the first step necessary to develop among teachers an interest in an objective study of religion in the public schools is to convince them that this may be a way to get at some of the facts about religion—to find out for themselves and to help children and youth make up their minds about the importance of religion, without undue pressure from religious enthusiasts. There is reason to believe that a great many teachers would welcome the opportunity to take specialized training designed to broaden their horizons in religious matters: to find out from firsthand contact with highly respected priests, ministers, and rabbis what they believe and why; to visit churches and synagogues as a part of an educational program to learn what happens in the different kinds of services and what the various practices mean; and to study, discuss, and compare the beliefs and practices of the different groups, attempting to discover their relevance, if any, to a satisfying life.

A second means of motivating teacher interest in the program proposed in this report is to invite teachers to participate in the initial consideration of the plan under the leadership of representative citizens who are earnestly seeking to improve public education. No teacher can be expected to welcome major responsibility for carrying out a program which others have planned without even considering his feelings in the matter. But if the plan as adopted by a given community grows out of months of serious study, discussion, and cooperative thinking by leading members of the board of education, the school faculty, the religious bodies, the PTA, the labor unions, and other community groups, it is safe to assume that the teachers who have been active in helping to formulate the plan will be equally enthusiastic about trying to make it succeed.

Finally, the board of education can further motivate teachers to participate in the program by three additional steps: first, by giving official assurance to the teachers that they will be protected from any personal opposition which might develop against them for their leadership in initiating the program in accordance with the policies democratically formulated; second, by providing salary increases or special bonuses to compensate the teachers for the time they spend in preparation for the assumption of this new responsibility; and third, by arranging for them to be excused from regular school duties to attend special lectures, forums, conventions, and other programs likely to strengthen their qualifications for effective leadership in the project. The board's thoughtfulness in this matter should, of course, be characteristic of its general policy throughout the school.

SELECTION OF TEACHERS TO LEAD

In one sense all teachers in each school engaged in this experiment should be participants. This does not mean that every teacher would be expected to provide for the study of religion in his classes, but it does mean that he should know what the experiment is and how it is to be carried on. It means, also, that all teachers in the school should be sincerely tolerant of the experiment—willing to have it undertaken and ready to cooperate with their fellow teachers in such details as scheduling excursions and arranging special assemblies when necessary.

In most cases teachers selected as leaders in the program would be those already teaching in the school. This would not mean that their teaching assignments would be changed. Teachers of literature selected as leaders in this program would continue to be teachers of literature, but they would work systematically to enrich the literature curriculum by integrating religious subject matter by the methods suggested in Chapter 2. The same procedure would be followed by teachers selected from the social studies field, from music, and from other areas of the curriculum. It is possible that in some communities outstanding teachers in "released-time" programs would be invited to join the public school staff, but of course only if they were certificated as fully qualified to teach in the public schools. It is strongly recommended that persons with "released-time" experience should not be employed to assist in this program unless there is strong evidence that they fully understand and approve the plan. Many teachers of sectarian religion, however sincere and effective in that area, would find it almost impossible to work satisfactorily as leaders in projects to study religion objectively. Such persons, if employed, should take the special training along with the other teachers in the public school in preparation for the initiation of the plan.

Those whose duty it is to select teachers to assume major responsibility for the success of the program should keep in mind the six qualifications discussed in the first main section of this chapter. Also, they should profit from the warning given by the American Council's Committee on Religion and Education as quoted on page 89, that two kinds of teachers may be dangerous: first, those who are uninformed in matters of religion and lack interest in learning; and second, those whose religious convictions are so deep that they might be inclined to attempt sectarian indoctrination. As to the actual methods of selecting teachers to lead, three suggestions are offered:

First, invite all the public school teachers who might

reasonably be expected to develop an interest in the project, to participate actively in all the preliminary planning as outlined in Chapter 5. Always leave the way open for these teachers to discontinue participation if they lose interest and for other teachers to join the planning groups if they care to do so.

Second, when the time comes to select teachers, opportunities should be given those who have worked persistently and helpfully in the preliminary planning to volunteer their leadership in the classroom to help put the plans into operation. If other teachers are needed, the superintendent of schools or his representative chosen to supervise the program should issue invitations to fill the remaining vacancies.

Third, no compulsion should be used to get teachers to assume this additional responsibility. It seems clear that unwilling teachers could not be helpful in this experiment.

It is to be hoped that this process of selection would bring together a teaching staff made up of representatives of the three major faiths in our country as well as those who hold no personal religious convictions.

THE WORKSHOP AS A METHOD OF TEACHER TRAINING

Most of the religious and educational leaders who are interested in experimentation with an objective study of religion in the public schools agree that ideally the teachers should receive their training as a part of their regular preparation in schools of education. Some of these leaders even insist that the task is so difficult that local communities would be unwise to try it without complete guidance from these institutions. For example, Morrison writes:

I seriously doubt that a community as such will get very far in meeting the delicate and intricate problems that will appear in the preparatory stage. These problems should be met first, it seems to me, in the schools regularly devoted to pedagogical training. When a curriculum, a set of texts and teachers trained in the techniques of dealing with this subject matter have been wrought out in this fashion, it will be time for the communities to take up the task.[15]

While agreeing that the method proposed by Morrison has many advantages, it is suggested here that teacher training institutions are unlikely to take the initiative in this matter until several communities become interested enough to try seriously to solve the problems alone. It is recommended that communities desiring to become pioneers in such a program start in a small way by using a special summer workshop as a means of providing their public school teachers with some basic training for undertaking the assignment. It is possible that this plan might even have certain advantages over the somewhat too theoretical consideration of the real problems which might characterize courses on this subject if they were offered in teachers colleges. In a special workshop organized to analyze the problems and to plan an experiment in the setting of a particular community, it seems certain that the most serious difficulties likely to arise in that place would inevitably be faced in a realistic manner.

Although it is unlikely that any two communities would follow exactly the same pattern in organizing workshops, the following suggestions are offered for the consideration of local leaders:

1. Basic training should be provided in a six weeks workshop to be held during the summer immediately preceding the beginning of actual experimentation in the school.

2. The best place for this workshop is in the community in which the experiment will take place, preferably in a centrally located public school building. If conditions make it impractical to hold the workshop within the local community, the second choice should be a college or university campus not too far away.

3. The major task of the workshop should be to formulate a definite plan for the first year of experimentation in the school. Very little study and discussion of the philosophy underlying the program would be possible in this short time, and it should not be necessary if the community preparation described in Chapter 5 has been successful.

4. The workshop program should include ample opportunity for interfaith fellowship and recreation as well as for study, discussion, and planning.

5. The workshop faculty should include well-qualified educators and religious leaders representing the Roman Catholic, Protestant, and Jewish faiths. Also, provision should be made to receive the benefit of constant criticisms from well qualified persons not identified with any religious group. At least one or two of the leaders should be residents of places outside the community in which the experiment is to be undertaken.

6. The details of the workshop should be planned far in advance and should be announced about three months before the opening date. This would be necessary to enable the participants to make their summer plans accordingly.

SUGGESTED CONTENTS OF THE FIRST WORKSHOP COURSE

The following outline is based upon four assumptions: first, that this summer workshop will last six weeks; second, that the participating public school teachers will be able to give it their full time; third, that these teachers have already been employed to teach in the school system in which the experiment is to take place; and fourth, that they have been officially selected to use this workshop to prepare themselves to assume the major responsibility for initiating and carrying on the experiment for at least one school year.

No attempt is made to present a bibliography for use in this workshop, but those responsible for the specific plans may want to make use of these chapters and the materials listed in the numerous footnotes. Also, a thorough understanding of the 1947 report of the American Council's Committee on Religion and Education should be a basic requirement.

The topics recommended for consideration are arranged in what is thought to be a logical order for study by the members of this workshop in which so much must be accomplished in such a short time.

1. *First week:*
   a. Moral confusion in our time.
   b. How character develops.
   c. The responsibility of community agencies for the moral character of the people.
   d. The challenge to the public school.
   e. The evolution of the local program of which this workshop is a part.
   f. The specific purposes of this workshop.
   g. A survey of proposed solutions to the problem of moral instability in America.
   h. The Committee on Religion and Education of the American Council on Education: Its origin, work, and 1947 report.
   i. Evaluations of this committee's 1947 report.

2. *Second week:*
   a. World religions: Main ones named, located geographically, and briefly described.
   b. The story of the Jews in history.
   c. The story of the Christian church.
   d. The rise and spread of secularism.
   e. Philosophies of religion: Main systems named, very briefly described, and identified with their leaders.
   f. The basic beliefs of the Roman Catholics, Protestants, Jews, and secularists.
   g. The struggle for religious liberty in America.
   h. Contemporary trends in religious thought in America.
   i. Laws and practices with reference to the relation of religion to public education: in the United States as a whole, in the various states, and in the state in which this experiment is to take place.

3. *Third week:*
   a. Some dangers to avoid in experimentation.
      (1) Creation of factional strife within the community.
      (2) Struggle for control of the public schools for purposes of sectarian indoctrination.
      (3) Denial of religious liberty of some of the people.
      (4) Tendency for the home and the church and synagogue to shift to the school all the responsibility for the religious education of the young.
   b. Some factors related to these dangers.
      (1) Sensitivity to the "felt needs" of all groups in planning the program.
      (2) Democratic participation in all phases of planning.
      (3) Widespread respect for the leaders in the program.
      (4) Qualifications of the teachers selected to lead.
      (5) Wise use of publicity.
   c. Methods of integrating religious subject matter into the curriculum of the public school.

4. *Fourth week:*
   a. Religious materials suitable for use in the public schools.
      (1) Kinds: Books and pamphlets, magazines, and audio-visual aids including the community itself.
      (2) Plans to insure effective use of all materials purchased.
   b. Intensive study and discussion of typical materials.
5. *Fifth week:*
   a. Visits to churches and synagogues, preferably in the community in which the experiment will take place:
      (1) To understand and appreciate the ways in which the people of each faith worship.
      (2) To develop personal friendships with one or more priests, rabbis, and ministers.
      (3) To become somewhat familiar with the total program of each of the major faiths.
      (4) To explore possible ways of increasing interfaith cooperation in the community.
   b. Examination of the programs of several outstanding public and private schools in which attention is already being given to a study of religion.
   c. Consideration of the formation of plans for the participating teachers to continue after the completion of the workshop to work individually or in small groups to improve their knowledge of religion.
6. *Sixth week:*
   a. Preparation of a tentative outline of plans for the first year of experimentation.
      (1) Main goals for the whole school.
      (2) Specific responsibilities of each teacher participating in the workshop.
      (3) Pupil participation in planning as the experiment is begun in the school.
      (4) Plans for in-service training and supervision throughout the year.

(5) Relationship of each participating teacher to other teachers, the superintendent, and the community respectively.

b. Formation of a specific plan to receive community reactions and consider them promptly.

c. Preparation of lists of materials to be recommended to the superintendent of schools for immediate purchase.

PROVISION FOR IN-SERVICE TRAINING AND SUPERVISION

It was suggested that during the last week of the summer workshop a plan should be formed to provide additional in-service training and supervision of the participating teachers throughout the first year of the experiment. It is strongly recommended that the leaders in this in-service program be selected from the summer workshop faculty. These supervisors would be expected to help the teachers whenever and however needed. Some possible aspects of this part of the plan might be:

1. To meet at least once each month with all the teachers actively cooperating in the experiment to hear reports of progress and to seek solutions to the problems encountered.

2. To help individual teachers both inside and outside the classroom whenever such help seems to be needed.

3. To keep teachers informed about radio programs, conventions, institutes, and new books and magazine articles which might prove useful to them.

4. To explore the possibilities of a cooperative arrangement with schools of education and religion in some nearby college or university by which specialists in these places would use the local school system as a permanent experi-

mental center to continue the project. This kind of arrangement could be expected to result in the expansion and improvement of the program in the local schools and to demonstrate to other teacher training institutions the part which they might play in preparing teachers for leadership in similar programs in other communities.

5 Community Preparation

Satisfactory community preparation for experimentation with an objective study of religion in the public schools requires that the community think its own way through the problems involved. There is no more certain guarantee of ultimate failure than for the community passively to accept a plan either superimposed from the outside or insisted upon by some special interest group within the community itself. The road which the people must travel in order to succeed in the proposed experiment is not an easy one, and it is to be expected that some communities will become discouraged and give up before getting very far along the way.

Among those who believe in the soundness of the proposals set forth by the American Council's Committee on Religion and Education there is not complete agreement as to the level at which experimentation should begin. Some people are of the opinion that any effective work on the problem must start at the top, in such groups as national organizations of religious and educational leaders and in schools of education willing to offer adequate training to the teachers who will at some future time assume local leadership. This project, on the other hand, is based upon the belief that success is most likely if sincere citizens at all levels—top leaders in many fields but also professional leaders and ordinary laymen in local communities—become interested in and work at the task simultaneously and cooperatively. It is not suggested that local leaders can reach a perfect solution to the problem alone. Rather, it is hoped that they can make some progress toward desirable goals and that the results of their efforts will prove useful to authorities seeking similar goals at higher levels. This means an acceptance of the educational philosophy stated by Bostwick in these words:

A school always has more problems than the principal can solve; it has more problems than the parents can solve. There is never a dearth of problems; there is only a dearth of intelligent, cooperative action directed toward their solution. If the school is to demonstrate the effectiveness of democracy as a way of life, then everyone concerned with a problem must have a part in thinking about it, in suggesting solutions, and in trying them out. This means parents, laymen, children, teachers, supervisors and administrators must be involved whenever their participation becomes necessary for the democratic solution of a problem.[1]

Also, when experiments concern controversial issues, it is particularly important for the people in each community to study and evaluate the problems involved and to help formulate the plans for action. Only in this way can they be expected to react constructively to the program when the experiment begins. Such a procedure helps the teachers too, since it insures community support. If the whole community pioneers together, it is reasonable to expect the whole community to cooperate to make the plan succeed; if the schools attempt to pioneer alone, it is unlikely that the community support will be strong.

The Lewin experiments in Iowa indicate that real democracy is not only a builder of good will but also can be an efficient method of operation, actually resulting in more production than is possible through autocratic or laissez faire methods.[2] Mort points out, however, that while democracy is one of the most vital of all educational principles, it is not the only one that must be considered; and it cannot be denied that sometimes other sound educational principles, such as simplicity and economy, inevitably limit the degree to which democracy can be practiced in actual situations.[3] Community leaders will find Part II of Mort's book on this subject a means of helping them to maintain what he calls a "common sense" balance between idealism and realism as they undertake an examination of the possible methods of local experimentation.[4] The Committee on Religion and Education does not insist that its conclusions be accepted but does urge that "educators, and also the lay public with whom the determination of educational policy ultimately rests in a democracy, approach this problem as objectively as the committee has tried to do in order that sound judgments may be reached."[5]

Local leaders interested in studying the committee's proposals and other possible solutions to the same problems should first of all face the question, Do the people in the community concerned really want more emphasis on or a better understanding of religion? Bower thinks that the typical answer to this question is likely to be in the affirmative. He writes:

It is not without significance that the problem in its present form does not arise merely or chiefly out of the interests of ecclesiastical groups. . . . On the contrary, it arises out of the concern of the community for the needs of the children and young people, on the one hand, and for the needs of the nation on the other.[6]

Freehof disagrees with Bower. While he himself is greatly concerned about the need for more attention to religion, he does not think that the people in general share his feeling. He believes that:

. . . secularist schools are precisely descriptive of society as it actually is. Society is secularist and the schools are secularist. . . . We, therefore, cannot claim widespread demand on the part of the *people* to overcome the non-religious nature of the public schools. We can only say that we church people are discontented with the secular nature of society, that we hope to change it and we try to persuade the government to let us change it by introducing the teaching of religion into the public schools.[7]

The committee does not entirely agree with either Bower or Freehof. Instead, it believes that when the meaning of its proposals is really understood by the people, some communities, but by no means all, will be interested in undertaking experimentation. Citizens desiring to classify their community as to its probable attitude on the subject might begin by asking and answering the following questions, at the same time considering the implications of each:

1. *Population:* Nationality and race groups represented and the percentage of each? Experiences in cooperation?

2. *Religion:* Membership in each religious faith represented? Experiences in cooperation among these religious groups and between them on the one hand and persons and groups not identified with organized religion on the other? Vitality of religious programs?

3. *Occupations:* Main kinds before, during, and since the war? The relationship of these facts to special problems in the community?

4. *Incomes:* Number of property-owners? Number on relief? General income level?

5. *Special problems:* Unemployment? Housing? Divorce? Juvenile delinquency? Recreational programs and facilities?

6. *Community reputation with reference to educational experimentation:* Pioneer? Early follower? Late follower? Laggard?

7. *Education:* Educational institutions in the community? General educational level of the people? Quality of books, magazines, and radio programs most popular with the people?

If an informal examination of this kind suggests to interested citizens that experimentation with an objective study of religion in the public schools might be acceptable to the people if the plan were understood, it is time to consider what steps should be taken to move in that direction. The remainder of this chapter is an attempt to outline in a logical order the essential phases of a program of study, discussion, and action which it is recommended that a community should include in the preparatory stage of the experiment.

UNOFFICIAL EXPLORATORY COMMITTEE

It is suggested that the first specific action be undertaken by an unofficial, self-appointed group of citizens, preferably both professional leaders and laymen. It would seem desirable to include in the nucleus of this group at least one highly respected leader of each of the three major faiths and one or more persons able to express the attitudes of typical citizens not affiliated with any religious group. This committee should work with the full knowledge and approval of the board of education and the superintendent of schools, and its formation might even be suggested by them; but it is probably best for educators not to be the main leaders in this initial stage of exploration. Their position of leadership at a later time will be much easier for them to assume if the initiation of the experiment has come mainly from outside the educational profession.

In addition to having a sincere interest in the problem, it

is important that the members of this group be genuinely
friendly among themselves. Petitt's following description of
an autonomous group might prove helpful here:

An autonomous group usually comes together principally because its members enjoy one another's companionship. The set
program which is the dominant note in formal education, and
also in many leisure-time programs, is of minor importance in
these less formal groups. The program of most adult education
and extension education, as well as of many recreation agencies,
is based upon the theory that the individual who joins a class
is attracted primarily by the activity. The individual is rarely
acquainted with others in such classes. However, in the autonomous groups existing in our society the dominant attraction is
the congeniality among acquaintances. The members of the
group know one another, like one another, and find satisfaction
in meeting together.

Sometimes the autonomous group is the result of some individual's awareness of a particular need or interest. Frequently
the pleasure of meeting together may be the chief motivating
factor, and programs and plans may develop later.[8]

It may be said that it is impossible in America today to
find communities in which such cooperative relationships
among leaders of the three major faiths can be expected. If
this contention is true, it is obvious that many of the proposals in this project are unrealistic. However, in some parts
of the country there is evidence that genuine cooperation is
possible. Rochester, New York, is reported to be one such
example. The Inter-Faith Goodwill Committee in that city
contains the most influential members of the three religious
groups, including a Catholic bishop and other Catholic officials of the diocese, three Jewish rabbis, four Protestant
ministers, and several laymen. Following are some excerpts
from a statement of this committee:

The Catholic, Protestant, and Jewish Communions in this city, through official representatives, have organized a permanent body known as the Inter-Faith Goodwill Committee to express their sense of comradeship and to consider such issues as may arise which are of common concern.

The confusion of the time offers to the members of these communions an opportunity to achieve a deeper understanding and appreciation of one another. It also challenges them to emphasize in their moral and religious outlook the great common principles which they believe to be the basis of our civilization. . . .

We welcome the public discussion of every question of common concern. We recognize that there are times when the public discussion of religious as well as political differences may be a necessity if our democracy is to function in a healthy way. . . .

We still have to make peace and avert another war. We have to organize our economy to provide for the needs of all without sacrificing our liberties to the tyranny of a police force. We have to find the types of education that will make man, as a spiritual being, master of the science and technology that, uncontrolled, will destroy him. We have to fight racial discrimination and a deadening secularism that denies the religious basis of life.

The differences in outlook that separate us are important. It is essential that we acknowledge and study them. But it would be tragic if in considering these differences we should drift into attitudes of hopeless antagonism toward one another. The religious and racial conflicts of the old world with their bitter consequences warn us against this danger. Along with the emphasis on differences, let there also be a common quest for a deeper understanding of the spiritual objectives of these great religious groups and their ways of life. From such understanding may come a new spiritual climate in which the work of all the communions may be more fruitful.[9]

As soon as interested citizens have come together as an unofficial exploratory committee to consider the various proposals for including a study of religion in public education, serious work can begin. This preliminary work should include at least four phases, each of which will be described briefly at this point.

1. The first phase consists of the study and discussion of basic books and pamphlets on the subject. It should not be necessary for every member of the group to read all the basic materials. However, it is strongly recommended that all begin by studying carefully at least these four works: Williams' *The New Education and Religion*,[10] Bower's *Church and State in Education*,[11] the American Council pamphlet on *The Relation of Religion to Public Education: The Basic Principles*,[12] and the NEA research bulletin entitled *The State and Sectarian Education*.[13] Next, the group should cooperate in examining and discussing the points of view presented in the following: Brubacher's *The Public Schools and Spiritual Values*,[14] Chave's *A Functional Approach to Religious Education*,[15] Moehlman's *School and Church: The American Way*,[16] Thayer's *Religion in Public Education*,[17] and perhaps some of the other materials included in the footnotes of this report. Also, in this initial stage two or three members of the group should be selected to consult the legal officials in the State Department of Education in the state concerned to get their assistance in understanding the full meaning of the constitutional provisions and the court decisions affecting the problem, as well as complete information on the actual practices.

It may be that the exploratory committee will want to go further into the background of the subject to increase its knowledge and also to prepare itself to recommend references to those who at a later time may assume responsibility as democratically chosen sponsors of experimentation. Some helps likely to serve these purposes are:

a. Background of the subject: Cubberley's *Public Education in the United States*,[18] Butts' *A Cultural History of Education*,[19] and Raup's *Education and Organized Interests in America*.[20]

b. Leadership in group work: Elliott's *The Process of Group Thinking*,[21] Tead's *The Art of Leadership*,[22] and the NEA's *Leadership at Work*.[23]

c. Materials to stimulate creativity in teachers: Two booklets of the Horace Mann-Lincoln Institute of School Experimentation entitled *The Teacher's Role in Pupil-Teacher Planning*[24] and *Guide to Study and Experimentation in Cooperative Planning in Education*,[25] Ohio State University's *Were We Guinea Pigs?*[26] Weber's *My Country School Diary*,[27] the Los Angeles City School's *Moral and Spiritual Values in Education*,[28] Chatto and Halligan's *The Story of the Springfield Plan*,[29] Chrietzberg's *The Story of Holtville*,[30] and Brameld's *Minority Problems in the Public Schools*.[31]

2. The second phase of the work suggested for the unofficial exploratory committee is to arrange and conduct several informal meetings to orient representatives of various groups in the community to the problem and to what experimentation in the local schools would mean. The invitation to attend these meetings should make it clear that their only purpose is to consider the desirability of choosing a thoroughly representative committee whose duties would be: to study the question further, to discuss the problem and the possible solutions with the people, and to submit a report including recommendations. To attempt to do more at this time would almost certainly be unwise. The groups represented in these meetings should include all organizations of the religious and educational leaders, the PTA, labor unions,

and others as necessary to insure expressions of opinion from a cross section of the population.

3. The next suggested duty of this committee concerns its official relationship to the board of education and the superintendent of schools. As indicated above, while educators probably should not be leaders in this preliminary survey of the possibilities, they should always be informed about and in agreement with each step taken. If this exploratory study produces reasonably strong evidence that the proposed experimentation in the public schools could be successful, the self-appointed committee should ask the board of education to state officially if it would be willing to give sincere consideration to the recommendations of a special committee provided such a group were democratically selected and instructed to analyze the problem in detail and submit a report.

4. If the board of education answers this question in the affirmative, the unofficial exploratory committee is ready to undertake the fourth and last phase of its work. This is the formation of such a representative committee. The board of education or its representatives should have a part in the selection of persons to serve in this more permanent group, which would now become the sponsoring committee. This committee should be requested to seek earnestly a satisfactory plan to include a study of religion in the public schools. At the same time, it should be made clear in the beginning that its task is to submit an honest report to the board of education even though that may mean a decision against the proposed experimentation.

THE SPONSORING COMMITTEE

The sponsoring committee should be clearly representative of all the people in the community. Also, it is imperative that

each member be a person who is respected by the group
which he represents. It may be that some or all members of
the unofficial exploratory committee should also serve with
this more permanent sponsoring group. Certainly local educators—administrators, curriculum specialists, classroom
teachers, and librarians—should be included. Finally, consideration should be given to the desirability of inviting in
one or more specialists in the fields of education and religion
who are known to be interested in this problem and well
qualified to serve as consultants. Such specialists might prove
very helpful even if they met with the group only occasionally
to offer their advice in matters of policy.

It is suggested that the duration of the sponsoring committee's assignment be a minimum of two years. During the
first year it should have three objectives: first, to analyze the
proposals for a study of religion in the local schools and
reach a tentative decision on what should be done; second,
if this decision is favorable to undertaking the experiment,
to plan and conduct a systematic educational program to
enable all the people to understand the proposal, to offer
their suggestions for the improvement of the plan, and to
express their wishes on going ahead with it; and third, to
submit to the board of education a complete report of the
committee's findings and recommend official action needed
by that body. During the second year the sponsoring committee's function should be to assist the board of education
and the public school faculty in various ways during the
initiation of the actual experimentation in the schools.

The committee's duties during its first year of existence
will be considered in the remainder of this chapter. Its later
responsibilities will be dealt with in Chapter 6.

The achievement of the sponsoring committee's first objective for its first year of existence requires a repetition of

the study and discussion engaged in earlier by the unofficial exploratory committee. This is described on page 113-115 and need not be repeated here.

The second objective of this committee should be to plan and conduct a community-wide educational program. This is a very difficult but important task, and failure in this undertaking would mean the defeat of the plan under consideration. The following suggested steps of procedure may be helpful:

1. Make a list of the many groups in the community for which education will need to be provided, and secure the names of their officers and other influential members. Consider the order in which these groups should be invited to study the proposals. The groups selected will not be exactly the same in all communities but probably in most places should include the organizations of religious leaders, lay religious groups, public school faculty, PTA, labor unions, business and professional men's clubs, business and professional women's clubs, YM and YW associations, and the children and youth of the junior and senior high school ages.

2. Consider what use should be made of the press, pulpit, and radio in the educational program. Very sound judgment on the subject of publicity is important since unwise action here might lead to unnecessary antagonism to the whole proposal.

3. Plan in detail the major points for emphasis in the program designed to help the people think their way through the problem. Include honest statements of the dangers as well as the possible advantages to be gained from the acceptance of the committee's proposals.

4. Give careful consideration to the personal qualities desirable in the leaders to be chosen for active participation in the community-wide program of study and discussion.

The function of these leaders is to help the people to find an answer to the question which they can correctly consider their own answer rather than to persuade them to accept in all its details the particular plan which the sponsoring committee has in mind.

5. Select a group of leaders to conduct this program, preferably persons who are members of the sponsoring committee. Hold a short institute to give them training for this responsibility. This training should include:

a. Information on what to say when leading groups.

b. Actual practice in saying it.

c. Emphasis on the proper attitudes to assume in the process of leading groups, particularly when objections are voiced.

d. Special plans for ascertaining the composition of each group to which the proposal is presented and for testing the reactions and recording questions and objections.

6. Schedule meetings for all the groups invited to study and discuss the proposal, and send trained leaders to meet with them. It is suggested that each cycle of meetings be followed by a general conference between the leaders on the one hand and the remaining members of the sponsoring committee on the other, to consider the results and to make necessary adjustments in the plan for future meetings with community groups. Whenever a real objection is discovered, the committee should try sincerely to find a solution satisfactory to the person to whom the objection is important.

7. Conduct a community poll on the proposed experimentation if and when it appears that a large majority of the people, including all such key groups as the religious leaders, the public school faculty, and the board of education, are favorable to proposals for experimentation. In addition to asking for an affirmative or negative vote, invite the people

to make short written statements on the reasons back of the choices expressed. Ballots and written statements should, of course, not be signed.

The last of the three objectives of the sponsoring committee for its first year is to submit to the board of education a detailed report of its activities, findings, and recommendations. This report should include in its section on findings all the essential facts growing out of the work of the committee so that the board will be able to make its own interpretation of the meaning of the data as well as to study the committee's conclusions. Future steps by the sponsoring committee will be dependent upon the board's response to its recommendations.

THE BOARD OF EDUCATION

If the board of education receives and approves recommendations which in the main follow the plan proposed throughout this report, the following steps of official action are suggested:

1. The board should authorize experimentation with an objective study of religion in part or all of the public school system for a minimum of one year, beginning with the opening of the next fall term.

2. It should instruct the superintendent of schools to appoint a member of the faculty, preferably one who is also a member of the sponsoring committee, to direct the experiment. This officer should act promptly along the lines suggested in Chapter 4 of this report to enlist teachers to lead in the experiment and to provide them with basic training by means of a summer workshop.

3. The board should offer its sincere cooperation in the experiment:

a. By assuring the teachers officially that they will be protected from any personal opposition which might develop against them for their leadership in the plan in accordance with the policies democratically arrived at and formally approved by the board;

b. By promptly announcing its intention of allowing salary increases or special bonuses to compensate teachers for the extra time and work required of those accepting positions of leadership in the program; and

c. By instructing the superintendent of schools to arrange for these teachers to be excused from their regular duties from time to time to attend meetings or to engage in other activities likely to improve their qualifications for this special responsibility.

4. The board should include in its budget adequate provision for the summer workshop to train the teachers, for the in-service program of training and supervision to continue throughout the year of experimentation, for the purchase of special equipment and supplies needed, and for the bonuses or salary increases promised the teachers.

If the approved plans call for the initiation of the experiment early in September, it is suggested that these four phases of official action by the board of education should necessarily be completed no later than the first week of the preceding April.

6 Expansion and Improvement With Experience

Several issues requiring careful analysis and the formulation of policies were introduced in Chapter 3. Chapters 4 and 5 were devoted to mapping a route along which it was suggested that a community should travel to prepare for local experimentation and to reach decisions which, though tentative and often theoretical, would be as realistic as they could be made by honest study, sincere attempts to appreciate the viewpoints of others, and democratic discussion. It is the purpose of Chapter 6 to provide for the reexamination of the whole plan during the first year of actual experimentation with an objective study of religion in the public schools, thus making possible the necessary changes in policy and procedure as soon as the need for such changes can be recognized by alert observers.

Also, in this chapter consideration will be given to the establishment of a permanent community educational council. This council would supersede the special sponsoring committee set up as an advisory group to assist with introducing a study of religion into the public schools. In addition to assuming the specific functions of this sponsoring committee, the community educational council would also undertake long-range planning to coordinate and improve the total educational program in the community. This seems desirable because the ultimate success of this as well as most

other educational projects in the local schools is to a great
extent dependent upon serious action by other community
agencies to improve their programs also. In a section entitled
"The Soil Which Grows Good Schools," Mort and Vincent
emphasize the fact that any vital improvement in the schools
"requires action by the public as a whole."[1] A detailed consideration of the work of a permanent community council
is not a part of this project. However, included in this final
chapter are some basic hints on how such a council might
be organized and what its relationship should be to the continued experimentation with a study of religion in the public
schools.

THE SPONSORING COMMITTEE

Probably the most difficult task of the sponsoring committee grows out of its leadership in the preparation of the
community for the experiment as described in Chapter 5.
If that duty has been wisely performed, the responsibilities
of this group during the first year of actual experimentation
in the schools should be comparatively simple. During the
year of preparation fairly detailed machinery for two-way
communication between the school staff and the people
outside the school will have been established. The aim now
should be to keep this machinery functioning. This is necessary for two reasons: first, to enable the teachers to get
prompt and intelligent assistance from the community in
proceeding with the experiment; and second, to keep open a
channel of communication by which the people outside the
school can easily and regularly report to the school staff their
reactions to the new program. The following specific sugges-

tions for keeping this communications machinery in operation are offered:

1. The sponsoring committee should include in its final preparation for the initiation of the experiment a plan by which every negative criticism would be immediately reported to the faculty member assigned to direct the program. All criticisms should be faced honestly and openly and necessary changes should be made and announced promptly. It is to be hoped that most of these changes could grow out of a careful consideration of each problem as it arises naturally in the in-service program of teacher training and supervision to continue throughout the year.

2. In addition to arranging for the school staff to receive and take prompt action on incidental criticisms directed at the experiment, the sponsoring committee should plan and conduct a community-wide survey sometime during the first year to determine the attitudes of the people toward the new program. This survey, like the poll of the preceding year, should offer citizens the opportunity to express their reasons for objections. The complete results should be made immediately available to the superintendent of schools and through him to the board of education.

3. The sponsoring committee should have a definite plan to keep the entire public school staff, the parents, and the religious leaders informed on the progress of the program and the problems connected with it. The cooperation of these groups should be enlisted particularly to simplify the procedures required to arrange for excursions and other special activities essential to the success of the program.

The other major responsibility suggested for the sponsoring committee during its second year of existence is to consider and, if it seems wise, to form a permanent community educational council. As stated above, this council would supersede the sponsoring committee but would greatly expand its work to include long-range planning and the coordination of the total educational program of the community. Perhaps the specific functions of the sponsoring committee in connection with the public school experiment in the objective study of religion should be assigned to a subcommittee of the new council.

The sponsoring committee and other leaders interested in considering the formation of a community educational council should begin by planning in a general way the steps to be taken in the process. The best procedures would depend upon the educational leadership available, but probably would include at least three main phases:

1. The first phase suggested is the thoughtful attempt to decide what kind of education is needed in the community concerned. Guidance in thinking about this subject can be found in the NEA discussion pamphlet on *Planning Postwar Education*,[2] the special education issue of *Survey Graphic* (November, 1947),[3] Mort and Vincent's *A Look at Our Schools*,[4] and the NEA's *Policies for Education in American Democracy*.[5] A study of materials of this kind might be expected to result in a tentative statement of several basic standards of what is considered to be satisfactory education. One graduate student made a careful analysis of the opinions of many educational leaders on this subject and finally concluded that educational programs suitable to the needs of most American communities must:

a. Operate under democratic control;

b. Deal with every aspect of modern living;

c. Support a structure of individual and social values;

d. Aim at assistance in the creation of a new and better world culture.[6]

2. A second step likely to prove helpful is the study of

several examples of educational projects promoted cooperatively by groups within communities or described by leading
educators as practical possibilities. Information about local
programs of this kind is included in Ogden and Ogden's
Small Communities in Action,[7] Brameld's *Design for America*,[8] the NEA's *Education for ALL American Youth*,[9] and
the NEA's *Spiritual Values in the Elementary School*.[10]

3. The last of these three suggested phases is actually to
organize a community educational council, making use of
typical procedures followed successfully in other places. Some
examples are described in the Public Affairs pamphlet *Youth
and Your Community*,[11] Koopman's *Utilizing the Local
Community*,[12] Olsen's *School and Community*,[13] and Sharp's
"School Public Relations Via a Community Council" in
The American School Board Journal (August, 1947).[14]

THE COMMUNITY EDUCATIONAL COUNCIL

If those interested in forming a community educational
council succeed in the achievement of their goal, there will
be many problems waiting for the attention of the new
organization. Most of these problems are likely to require
considerable time for study, discussion, and planning before
definite recommendations can be made or any other specific
action taken. The authors of *School and Community* believe
that community councils should be mainly advisory. They
write:

A council is primarily an advisory and catalytic influence,
rather than a super administrative agency. Its purpose is to
clarify community problems and needs and to stimulate existing
individual agencies to more intelligent and cooperative efforts
in meeting those problems and needs.[15]

While effective councils will examine all kinds of educational problems and will encourage cooperative action to solve them, in this report attention will be given to only four specific long-range goals, each of which is related to the public school experimentation with an objective study of religion.

1. One of these long-range goals is the encouragement of teacher training institutions to assume the major responsibility for preparing teachers for effective leadership in programs to study religion objectively in the public schools. Responsibility for systematic planning and action leading to this result might be assumed by the council as a whole or by its appropriate subcommittee.

It must be admitted that success in this undertaking may be extremely difficult, and certainly it is unrealistic to expect an immediate response from typical state teachers colleges. As indicated before in this report, many people feel that all experimentation of the kind outlined in this project should be initiated at high levels. Applied to this problem, this contention means that it is a waste of time for local community councils to attempt anything so difficult as persuading tax-supported teacher training institutions to cooperate in such a project. Brunner, for example, thinks that attempts to encourage cooperation by teachers colleges

would properly fall to the lot of some national agency like the American Council on Education. Publishers and teacher training institutions are not going to listen to a single community or even to a scattered sample of these. The pressures on them are entirely too many and too frequent for them to pay much attention to this sort of thing.[16]

If the local council discovers that Brunner's opinion on this subject is correct, it might decide to attempt to find ways to accomplish the same purpose by offering to finance such a program under the direction of one or more educational institutions. An example comparable to this is the new inter-group relations program started in September, 1948, under the direction of Teachers College, Columbia University, but financed for five years by the National Conference of Christians and Jews. It seems reasonable to believe that this kind of procedure, even though undertaken by one community on a very small scale, might lead to making the local school system into a laboratory for educational experimentation through a cooperative agreement with schools of education and religion in a near-by college or university as suggested on pages 104-105.

2. A second possible project for the local council to consider is to urge authors of school textbooks to include religious subject matter wherever it seems naturally to belong when revising existing books or writing new ones. The quotation from Brunner on the preceding page applies as much to publishers and authors of textbooks as to the policymaking authorities in charge of tax-supported teacher training institutions.

If sincere attempts to reach this objective make it clear that satisfactory results cannot be expected, perhaps the local council may be able to act independently in this area too. It was suggested above that independent financing be used to provide a cooperative plan to make the local school system a laboratory for educational experimentation under the guidance of well-qualified educational and religious leaders. If this plan is followed, perhaps the experiment could be expanded to include the preparation of one or more textbooks, probably over a period of several years. This would have the advantage always inherent in allowing textbooks to grow out of the actual classroom practices of good teachers.

Such textbook or textbooks, once completed, could be offered for use in other schools desiring to experiment. Evidence that such a procedure can succeed has been supplied by McCasland of the University of Virginia, who followed a plan similar to this in writing *The Bible in Our American Life.*[17] This is a nonsectarian high school text developed out of the author's experience in teaching the materials included. It has now been published in mimeographed form and is used in many public high schools.

3. Another long-range goal is the development of satisfactory methods of evaluating the results of experimentation with a study of religion in the public schools. This is another challenging task which might be undertaken by a carefully selected committee of the community educational council. Members of this committee should be persons trained in the field of education and interested particularly in character education.

Obviously, before attempting to evaluate the results of the program in operation in the local schools the leaders should recall the aims for which the experiment was undertaken. These were discussed on pages 33-37 and might be summarized as follows:

a. To discourage attempts to put into operation various schemes which a careful examination would classify as undesirable or even dangerous.

b. To remove the antireligious effect resulting from the public school practice of minimizing the role of religion in the culture.

c. To develop religious literacy by helping children and youth to acquire a knowledge of religion.

d. To strengthen the emphasis on moral and spiritual values by developing an understanding of why these values are important.

e. To increase the unity among Americans by building

better intergroup understanding and appreciation in contrast to mere tolerance.

It is to be hoped, of course, that even the partial achievement of these goals would ultimately lead to more desirable ways of living and behaving. Attempts to evaluate the success of the program should include plans to examine evidence of progress toward each of the five objectives and also to discover signs of growth toward this ultimate goal.

It must be admitted that far too little is known about how to measure character development. The following opinions and emphases considered important by several educators interested in this general objective may be worthy of examination by committee members desiring to consider the possibilities in this area:

a. Sands writes:

It is indeed impossible to measure that which is unexpressed, such as sensations of inspiration and depression, visions of totality in life, and emotional impressions. Yet these are the fabric of spiritual life, they have a positive reality, and to some degree they are revealed in the visible and audible reactions of the individual to the outer world. To make any approach toward evaluation of spiritual values we must assume that the spiritual life of a person is expressed at least in part through his observable conduct—his actions and language.[18]

With this statement as a basic assumption, Sands goes on to list several criteria for an evaluation of spiritual status and progress. It is difficult to see how he could be very objective in his measurements, and he does not claim that the methods which he suggests are highly accurate.

b. Ligon feels more certain that satisfactory evaluation is possible, and he believes that he has real evidence to prove the soundness of his system of character education. In his introductory statement on this subject he writes:

Since the aim of character education is the formation of attitudes, measures of success must consist of attitude scales. One of the reasons for our very slow progress in character education is the fact that we seldom make any systematic effort to test the effectiveness of our methods.[19]

He then names and describes the three following methods of measuring attitudes:

(1) Thurstone method. This is very technical and difficult to score, but is considered the most accurate of the three.

(2) Logical graphic scale.

(3) Systematic short-interval observations of the behavior of children during free play periods.

Ligon's scales include elements of all three methods, with major emphasis on the first two.

c. Attempts by leaders in Springfield, Massachusetts, to evaluate the Springfield Plan have been somewhat incidental, but interesting. They are described by Chatto and Halligan in their book *The Story of the Springfield Plan.*[20]

d. A teacher of literature who for many years has tried to measure ideals as developed in his classes describes the bases of his plan in the following words:

I first freed myself from grade equivalents and percentiles and invented a scale of values. . . . For ten years now I have not given an examination in literature. . . .

If, as Ulrich of Harvard writes, "all good teaching consists in changing passivity into activity," then my purpose was to use literature in such a manner as to make a difference in the behavior of the pupils, but conduct could not be a goal unless I looked for it, held pupils responsible for it, graded it—that is, measured it.[21]

e. Finally, Bowen writes from the viewpoint of a supervisor who attempts to evaluate what is happening to children spiritually as a result of a program of education designed to strengthen character. She uses four methods of testing:

(1) Observation as an outsider.

(2) Observation as a participant in the pupil-teacher group.

(3) Conferences with teachers.

(4) Analyses of anecdotal and cumulative records.[22]

4. The last of the four long-range problems suggested for the consideration of the community educational council concerns private and parochial schools. In the opinion of the author of Chapter 5 of *The Public Schools and Spiritual Values,*

It is all very well to speak to parents of the broader social contacts that the child will make in the public school, and tell them that such broad contacts will make for social unity and democracy. It is the very broadness of the contacts that frightens them, for they would not have their children, if they can help it, exposed to an environment where unpleasantness and socially undesirable characteristics at the least, and positively immoral behavior at the worst, may be acquired. It is not always indefensible snobbery that leads parents to an undemocratic decision; more frequently it is fear.

Private and parochial schools were established at a time when there were no adequate public schools, and their continuance is a criticism of the public school; as the public schools improve, however, the need of private and church enterprise in education will diminish.[23]

In a *Harper's Magazine* article by Lynes on the subject of private schools a similar emphasis is present. The author says that the best of the nonpublic schools in America have four advantages over the public schools: first, teaching under optimum conditions; second, individual attention to pupils' needs; third, training in manners and all it connotes; and fourth, grounding in religion.[24]

It may be that the community educational councils in some places would be interested in undertaking seriously the task of making public education so satisfactory in all these respects that many of the people now supporting private schools would no longer consider such additional expenditures necessary. The achievement of this goal would not only save parents the cost of nonpublic education, but it would also bring much needed pressure from these parents for the further improvement of the public schools. Parochial schools, which are established and maintained to encourage children to accept and become loyal adherents of a particular religious faith, would, of course, be unaffected by this program. Also, it is probable and perhaps desirable that a small number of other private schools would continue to exist. Such schools, particularly if well financed, could serve a useful purpose as educational laboratories.

THE PUBLIC SCHOOL TEACHERS

When the experimentation proposed in this report has been started in a public school system, the main responsibility for its success must be assumed by the teachers assigned to positions of leadership. In this section attention will be given to three important phases of their part in the general plan to expand and improve the program:

1. The first of these phases consists of emphasis on the fact that each of these teachers should take seriously the assignment which he has agreed to accept. This necessitates:

a. A clear understanding of the objectives, methods, and dangers of the program as described here.

b. A persistent and intelligent effort to measure up to the standards for teachers as presented on pages 90-94.

c. Constant attention to the very difficult task of presenting fairly the opposing points of view of different religious groups.

d. Systematic study by each teacher to improve his qualifications for leadership in the program.

e. Daily search for new and better materials for the curriculum and for more meaningful ways in which to use them.

f. Major emphasis on one new project at a time. Any teacher responsible for leadership in one or two successful innovations during the first year of this program will have made a distinct contribution in the experiment.

2. The next phase of the responsibility to be assumed by the teachers concerns their relationship to the community. Several specific suggestions on this subject may be helpful:

a. Be democratic. The teacher who is known to be genuinely democratic in all his community contacts will be trusted to play fair in the school, even when controversial issues are involved.

b. Invite criticisms and face critics. Wise teachers who lead in this program will freely admit the difficulty of the task and will invite suggestions and criticisms from all who are interested. When negative criticisms come, they will do their best to meet the critics face to face and try to find acceptable solutions to the problems involved.

c. Develop new and strong personal friendships among both laymen and officials of all religious faiths represented in the community and also among citizens not affiliated with any religious group. Discuss with those persons best qualified to help, any special problems which arise in the experiment, and try sincerely to test their suggestions which seem to be sound. Always give full credit to the persons from whom helpful suggestions come.

d. Become familiar with acceptable principles of public relations for teachers and practice them consistently. Basic help of this kind can be found in the pamphlet *Public Relations for Rural and Village Teachers*.[25]

3. The last of the three kinds of teacher responsibility to be considered here is effective cooperation with other leaders in the program and with the public school staff not leading in the experiment. This means:

a. Thoughtfulness in requesting cooperation from the public school staff not specifically assigned to leadership in the program. This would include such persons as janitors and bus drivers as well as teachers, supervisors, and librarians.

b. Willing cooperation with the public school staff members who are not leaders in this program but who are engaged in other kinds of educational experimentation.

c. Readiness to assist the community educational council to move forward toward its goals, including such projects as the four long-range objectives described on pages 126-132.

d. Consistent and intelligent effort to plan through the in-service training program for the future success of the experiment. One suggested activity for this in-service training group is to formulate and present to the superintendent of schools a specific proposal for the future improvement of the program. As indicated previously, it is to be hoped that such a plan would involve active cooperation with the educational and religious leadership in a nearby college or university.

THE SUPERINTENDENT OF SCHOOLS

The responsibilities of the superintendent of schools with respect to the success of this experiment are similar to his duties in connection with any other kind of educational experimentation in the schools. Typical of these duties are the following:

1. To delegate authority wisely to the persons responsible for the administration and supervision of the program, standing ready to offer his personal assistance whenever it is needed.

2. To cooperate with the community educational council, assisting it in every way possible to understand and work intelligently toward goals which are educationally sound and designed to meet the needs of the community.

3. To help the board of education to understand its responsibility for the success of the program, particularly its obligation to establish and maintain policies insuring freedom from insecurity among teachers who accept positions of leadership in the experiment.

4. To report to the board of education at regular intervals on the success of the program, recommending such official action as these reports suggest to be best.

Footnotes

[1] Harold Laski, *Faith, Reason, and Civilization* (New York, The Viking Press, 1944), p. 28.

[2] G. Bromley Oxnam, *et al.*, "Are We Losing Our Moral Standards?" *Town Meeting*, XIII (February 24, 1948), p. 13.

[3] *Ibid.*, p. 6.

[4] *Ibid.*, p. 6.

[5] Eduard C. Lindeman, "The Enduring Goal," *Survey Graphic*, XXXVI (November, 1947), p. 639.

[6] Eduard C. Lindeman, "Sources of Value for Modern Man," *Religious Education*, XLII (September–October, 1947), p. 286. Used by permission of *Religious Education*, 20 West Jackson Boulevard, Chicago 4, Illinois.

[7] Stanley High, "Our Schools Need More Than Money," *The Reader's Digest*, XXVI (December, 1947), p. 16

[8] Eduard C. Lindeman, "The Enduring Goal," *Survey Graphic*, XXXVI (November, 1947), p. 640.

[9] Reinhold Niebuhr, "The Impact of Protestantism Today," *The Atlantic Monthly*, CLXXXI (February, 1948), p. 59.

[10] *Ibid.*, p. 61.

[11] Hedley S. Dimock, "The Character Education of the Adolescent," *Religious Education*, XLII (July–August, 1947), p. 241. Used by permission of *Religious Education*, 20 West Jackson Boulevard, Chicago 4, Illinois.

[12] *The Constitution of the United States.* Amendments to the Constitution, Article I.

[13] American Council on Education, *The Relation of Religion to Public Education: The Basic Principles*, A Report Prepared by the Committee on Religion and Education (Washington, D. C., American Council on Education, 1947), p. iii.

[14] *Ibid.*, p. 29.

[15] Charles Clayton Morrison, "Protestantism and the Public Schools," *The Christian Century*, XLIII (April 17, 1946), pp. 490–492.

[16] American Council on Education, *op. cit.*, pp. 20–21.

[17] *Ibid.*, p. 31.

[18] Supreme Court of the United States, *People of the State of Illinois ex rel. Vashti McCollum, Appellant, v Board of Education of School District No. 71, Champaign County, Illinois et al: Appeal from the*

Supreme Court of the State of Illinois (No. 90, October Term, 1947–March 8, 1948), pp. 4–5 in section headed "Mr. Justice Jackson, concurring."

CHAPTER 1

[1] Ellwood P. Cubberley, *The Public Education in the United States* (New York, Houghton-Mifflin Company, 1934), p. 233.

[2] Reinhold Niebuhr, "Our Relations to Catholicism," *Christianity and Crisis*, VII (September 15, 1947), p. 5.

[3] Eduard C. Lindeman, "The Enduring Goal," *Survey Graphic*, XXXVI (November, 1947), p. 638.

[4] William Clayton Bower, *Church and State in Education* (Chicago, The University of Chicago Press, 1944), pp. 6–7.

[5] Charles Clayton Morrison, "The Inner Citadel of Democracy," *The Christian Century*, LVIII (May 7, 1941), p. 654.

[6] American Council on Education, *op. cit.*, p. 53.

[7] Statement by Harrison S. Elliott, personal interview.

[8] William Lewis Troyer, "Christian Nurture and Recent Social Science Investigation." *Religious Education*, XLII (November–December, 1947), pp. 351–356. Used by permission of *Religious Education*, 20 West Jackson Boulevard, Chicago 4, Illinois.

[9] Harry Emerson Fosdick, *The Meaning of Faith* (New York, Association Press, 1917), p. 85.

[10] National Education Association, *Education for ALL American Youth*, Prepared by the Educational Policies Commission (Washington, D. C., National Education Association, 1944), p. 145.

[11] *Ibid.*, p. 146.

[12] *Ibid.*, p. 146.

[13] *Ibid.*, p. 146.

[14] *Ibid.*, p. 147.

[15] J. Paul Williams, *The New Education and Religion* (New York, Association Press, 1946), pp. 14–15.

[16] Reprinted from *Education for Modern Man* by permission of Dial Press, Inc., copyright 1946 by Sidney Hook, p. 108.

[17] *Ibid.*, p. 109.

[18] *Ibid.*, p. 109.

[19] Charles Clayton Morrison, "Protestantism and the Public Schools," *The Christian Century*, XLIII (April 17, 1946), p. 492.

[20] Roma Gans, "Teachers Appraise Supervision and Administration," *Education*, LXVII (December, 1946), p. 221.

[21] John L. Childs, "Spiritual Values in Public Education," *Teachers College Record*, XLVIII (March, 1947), p. 367.

[22] Harold V. Baker, "Spiritual Values Give Life Its Highest Meaning," *NEA Journal*, XXXVI (December, 1947), p. 629.

[23] John S. Brubacher (ed.), *The Public Schools and Spiritual Values*, (New York, Harper & Brothers, 1944), pp. 146–152.

[24] Harry Emerson Fosdick, "Shall American School Children Be Religiously Illiterate?" *School and Society*, LXVI (November 29, 1947), p. 402.

[25] From *Principles of School Administration*, by Paul R. Mort. 1946. Courtesy of McGraw-Hill Book Co., p. 42.

[26] Alice V. Keliher, "No Monopoly on Leadership," *Educational Leadership*, IV (January, 1947), p. 216.

[27] Brubacher (ed.), *op. cit.*, p. 144.

[28] American Council on Education, *op. cit.*, pp. 45–46.

[29] Bower, *op. cit.*, p. 74.

[30] *Ibid.*, p. 75.

[31] American Council on Education, *Religion and Public Education*, A Report of a Conference Called by the American Council on Education with the Cooperation of the National Conference of Christians and Jews (Princeton, New Jersey, 1944), pp. 32–33.

[32] V. T. Thayer, *Religion in Public Education* (New York, The Viking Press, 1947), pp. 4–6.

[33] American Council on Education, *The Relation of Religion to Public Education: The Basic Principles*. A Report Prepared by the Committee on Religion and Education (Washington, D. C., American Council on Education, 1947), p. 24.

[34] *Ibid.*, p. vi.

[35] Harry Emerson Fosdick, "Shall American School Children Be Religiously Illiterate?" *School and Society*, LXVI (November 29, 1947), p. 402.

[36] Howard J. Howson, "The Curricular Approach to Religious Prejudice," (Unpublished report of a study conducted for the National Conference of Christians and Jews, 1942–43, available in Vassar College Library), p. 46.

[37] *Ibid.*, pp. 47–49.

[38] *Ibid.*, p. 55.

[39] *Ibid.*, p. 55.

[40] *Ibid.*, p. 100.

CHAPTER 2

[1] William Lyon Phelps, *Human Nature in the Bible* (New York, Charles Scribner's Sons, 1922), p. ix.

[2] C. Leslie Glenn, "Why I Read the Bible," *Atlantic Monthly*, CLXXVI (September, 1945), p. 63.

[3] National Education Association, *op. cit.*, p. 148.

[4] American Council on Education, *The Relation of Religion to Public Education: The Basic Principles*, A Report Prepared by the Committee on Religion and Education (Washington, D. C., American Council on Education, 1947), p. 32.

[5] Lucille Desjardins, "Resources for Religious Education," *The International Journal of Religious Education*, XI (October, 1934), p. 22.

[6] Harry Emerson Fosdick, *The Meaning of Faith* (New York, Association Press, 1917), p. 250.

[7] Caroline Miles Hill (ed.), *The World's Great Religious Poetry* (New York, The Macmillan Company, 1923).

[8] Archer Wallace, *The Religious Faith of Great Men* (New York, Round Table Press, 1934).

[9] Lawrence E. Nelson, *Our Roving Bible* (New York, Abingdon–Cokesbury Press, 1945).

[10] National Education Association, "Personal Growth Leaflets" (Leaflets published for sale at cost by the Hugh Birch–Horace Mann Fund, National Education Association, Washington, D. C.).

[11] American Bible Society, *The Influence of the English Bible upon the English Language and upon English and American Literature* (New York, American Bible Society), p. 10.

[12] *Ibid.*, p. 19.

[13] *Ibid.*, p. 24.

[14] S. Vernon McCasland, *The Bible in Our American Life*, pp. 176–181. Used by permission of the Virginia Council of Churches, Inc.

[15] *Ibid.*, pp. 191–195.

[16] Lenore Cohen, *Bible Tales for Very Young Children*, Vols. I and II (Cincinnati: The Union of American Hebrew Congregations, 1934–36).

[17] Walter R. Bowie, *The Story of the Bible* (New York, The Abingdon Press, 1934).

[18] Muriel Streibert Curtis, *The Story of the Bible People* (New York, The Macmillan Company, 1942).

[19] Hendrick W. Van Loon, *The Story of the Bible* (New York, Boni and Liveright, 1923).

[20] Sophia L. Fahs, *Jesus, the Carpenter's Son* (Boston, The Beacon Press, 1946).

[21] Florence W. Klaber, *Joseph* (Boston, The Beacon Press, 1941).

[22] John W. Flight, *Moses* (Boston, The Beacon Press, 1942).

[23] Walter R. Bowie, *Great Men of the Bible* (New York, Harper & Brothers, 1936).

[24] H. V. Morton, Women of the Bible (New York, Dodd, Mead, and Company, 1941).

[25] American Bible Society, "Forty Favorite Chapters in Your Bible," A list on a card for daily Bible reading (New York, American Bible Society).

[26] Letter from Robert Allen, Assistant in Curriculum, Public Schools, Louisville, Kentucky, January 19, 1948.

[27] Radio Department, The Congregational Christian Churches, 287 Fourth Avenue, New York 10, N. Y.

[28] Edgar J. Goodspeed, The Junior Bible (New York, The Macmillan Company, 1936).

[29] Wilbur Owen Sypherd, The Book of Books (New York, Alfred A. Knopf Company, 1944).

[30] Lewis Browne, The World's Great Scriptures (New York, The Macmillan Company, 1946).

[31] Lewis Browne, The Graphic Bible (New York, The Macmillan Company, 1929).

[32] Mary Ellen Chase, The Bible and the Common Reader (New York, The Macmillan Company, 1945).

[33] Edgar J. Goodspeed, How to Read the Bible (Philadelphia, The John C. Winston Company, 1946).

[34] Edgar J. Goodspeed, The Story of the Bible (Chicago, The University of Chicago Press, 1936).

[35] Donald Attwater, A Catholic Dictionary (New York, The Macmillan Company, 1941).

[36] M. W. Jacobus, E. C. Lane, and A. C. Zenos, A New Standard Bible Dictionary (New York, Funk and Wagnalls Company, 1938).

[37] Anne Lloyd Basinger, "Religion at Brearley," The Brearley Bulletin, XX (December, 1944), p. 10.

[38] Letter from Robert Allen, Assistant in Curriculum, Public Schools, Louisville, Kentucky, January 19, 1948.

[39] Florence M. Fitch, Their Search for God (New York, Lothrop, Lee and Shepard Company, 1947).

[40] Edna M. Baxter, How Our Religion Began (New York, Harper & Brothers, 1939).

[41] Joseph Gaer, How the Great Religions Began (New York, Robert M. McBride and Company, 1929).

[42] Charles Samuel Braden, The World's Religions (Nashville, The Cokesbury Press, 1939).

[43] Robert M. Hume, The World's Living Religions (New York, Charles Scribner's Sons, 1924).

[44] Lewis Browne, This Believing World (New York, The Macmillan Company, 1929).

[45] Lewis Browne, *The World's Great Scriptures* (New York, The Macmillan Company, 1946).

[46] C. A. Hauser, *Teaching Religion in the Public School* (New York, Round Table Press, 1942.

[47] "Data Bulletin—Tenth Grade Social Studies," Prepared by County Committee Assisted by Staff Members from the U.S. Office of Education (Issued by Montgomery County, Rockville, Maryland, September, 1941), Table of Contents.

[48] Frances Nall, "Correlating the Curriculum of the Church and School," *Religious Education*, XXXVII (September–October, 1942), p. 290. Used by permission of *Religious Education*, 20 West Jackson Boulevard, Chicago 4, Illinois.

[49] Ethel L. Smither, *A Picture Book of Palestine* (New York, Abingdon–Cokesbury Press, 1947).

[50] Roland H. Bainton, *The Church of Our Fathers* (New York, Charles Scribner's Sons, 1941).

[51] Lucille Desjardins, *Our Living Church* (Philadelphia, The Westminster Press, 1936).

[52] Reginald D. Manwell and Sophia L. Fahs, *The Church Across the Street* (Boston, The Beacon Press, 1947).

[53] George Hedley, *The Christian Heritage in America* (New York, The Macmillan Company, 1947).

[54] William W. Sweet, *The Story of Religion in America* (New York, Harper & Brothers, 1939).

[55] Ralph D. Owen, *Learning Religion from Famous Americans* (New York, The Macmillan Company, 1927).

[56] Wallace, *op. cit.*

[57] George School, "Religion at George School," *George School Bulletin*, XVIII (March, 1947), p. 12.

[58] Letter from Erdman Harris, Headmaster, Shady Side Academy, Pittsburgh, Pennsylvania, December 24, 1947.

[59] Florence M. Fitch, *One God: The Ways We Worship Him* (New York, Lothrop, Lee and Shepard Company, 1944).

[60] Manwell and Fahs, *op. cit.*

[61] Louis Finkelstein, J. Elliott Ross, and William Adams Brown, *The Religions of Democracy* (New York, Devin–Adair Company, 1946).

[62] McCasland, *op. cit.*

[63] Mildred Moody Eakin, *Getting Acquainted with Jewish Neighbors* (New York, The Macmillan Company, 1945).

[64] Milton Steinberg, *Basic Judaism* (New York, Harcourt, Brace and Company, 1947).

[65] Benson Y. Landis (ed.), *Religion and the Good Society* (New York, The National Conference of Christians and Jews, 1943).

[66] Roger Williams Straus, *Religious Liberty and Democracy* (New York, Willett, Clark and Company, 1939).

[67] H. Martin, P. Davidson, *Good Christian Men* (New York, Charles Scribner's Sons, 1940).

[68] Paul Douglass and Edmund deS. Brunner, *The Protestant Church as a Social Institution* (New York, Harper & Brothers, 1935).

[69] John H. Elliott, *Building Bridges* (New York, The National Conference of Christians and Jews, 1947).

[70] United Christian Youth Movement, *Christian Youth and Interfaith Cooperation* (Chicago, The United Christian Youth Movement, 1944).

[71] McCasland, *op. cit.*

[72] William DeWitt Hyde, *The Five Great Philosophies* (New York, The Macmillan Company, 1913).

[73] Edward Hazen Foundation, "Hazen Books on Religion" (distributed by the Association Press, New York, 1936–45).

[74] Letter from Frank D. Ashburn, Headmaster, Brooks School, North Andover, Massachusetts, December 14, 1947.

[75] George School, *op. cit.*, pp. 13–14.

[76] Frank Eakin and Mildred Moody Eakin, *Let's Talk about Our Religion* (New York, The Macmillan Company, 1944).

[77] McCasland, *op. cit.*

[78] William Clayton Bower, *The Living Bible* (New York, Harper & Brothers, 1936).

[79] Abraham Cronbach, *The Bible and Our Social Outlook* (Cincinnati, The Riverdale Press, 1941).

[80] Charles Duell Kean, *Christianity and the Cultural Crisis* (New York, Association Press, 1945).

[81] Frank Glenn Lankard, *The Bible Speaks to Our Generation* (New York, Oxford University Press, 1941).

[82] Arthur C. Wickenden, *Youth Looks at Religion* (New York, Harper & Brothers, 1939).

[83] Harry Emerson Fosdick, *The Meaning of Faith* (New York, Association Press, 1917), p. 170.

[84] McCasland, *op. cit.*, p. 150.

[85] Hauser, *op. cit.*, p. 171.

[86] Sophia L. Fahs, *Beginnings of Earth and Sky* (Boston: The Beacon Press, 1937).

[87] James B. McKendry, "Correlation of Week-day Religious Education with the Public School Program," *Religious Education*, XLII (July–August, 1947), p. 205. Used by permission of *Religious Education*, 20 West Jackson Boulevard, Chicago 4, Illinois.

[88] McCasland, *op. cit.*, p. 152.

[89] Sophia L. Fahs and Dorothy T. Spoerl, *Beginnings of Life and Death* (Boston, The Beacon Press, 1938).

[90] Robert L. Calhoun, *What Is Man?* (New York, Association Press, 1939).

[91] Hauser, *op. cit.*, p. 179.

[92] Bertha Stevens, *Child and Universe* (New York, The John Day Company, 1931).

[93] Bertha Stevens, *How Miracles Abound* (Boston, The Beacon Press, 1941).

[94] McKendry, *op. cit.*, p. 204.

[95] George School, *op. cit.*, p. 12.

[96] Conrad A. Houser, *Latent Religious Resources in Public School Education* (Philadelphia, The Heidelberg Press, 1924).

[97] Verna Hillis, *Martin and Judy*, Vol. I (1939); Verna Hillis and Sophia L. Fahs, *Martin and Judy*, Vols. II and III (Boston, The Beacon Press, 1940 and 1943).

[98] Baxter, *op. cit.*

[99] Eakin and Eakin, *op. cit.*

[100] Alberta Munkres, *Which Way for Our Children?* (New York, Charles Scribner's Sons, 1936).

[101] Wickenden, *op. cit.*

[102] Lewis Joseph Sherrill, *The Opening Doors of Childhood* (New York, The Macmillan Company, 1939).

[103] Hill, *op. cit.*

[104] John Macmurray, *The Structure of Religious Experience* (New Haven, Yale University Press, 1936).

[105] William Clayton Bower, *Church and State in Education* (Chicago, The University of Chicago Press, 1944), p. 32.

[106] Federal Council of the Churches of Christ in America, "Church and State—Some Current Issues," *Information Service*, XX (November 15, 1941), Section entitled "The Indianapolis Experiment."

[107] Louisville Public Schools, *Tentative Course of Study, MUSIC, Junior High Schools*, Issued by the Division of Curriculum and Research (Louisville, Kentucky, Louisville Public Schools, 1947), pp. 16, 17, 36.

[108] Los Angeles City Schools, *Moral and Spiritual Values in Education*, Issued by the Curriculum Section, but produced cooperatively by many groups within the community (Los Angeles, Los Angeles City Schools, 1944–45), p. 46.

[109] *Ibid.*, pp. 50–53.

[110] Louisville Public Schools, *op. cit.*, pp. 28, 52.

[111] From *Christ and the Fine Arts*, by Cynthia Pearl Maus, p. 23. Published by Harper & Brothers, New York 16, N. Y. Used by special permission of the author.

[112] Fred Eastman (ed.), *Ten One-Act Plays* (Chicago, Willet, Clark and Company, 1937).

[113] Brady School, *Brady School Plan for Character and Citizenship Training* (Written by Mary C. Sullivan, Principal of Brady School, 2920 Joy Road, Detroit 6, Michigan; published by The Wines Printing Company, Detroit, Michigan, 1947).

[114] *Ibid.*, p. 6.

[115] *Ibid.*, p. 5.

[116] *Ibid.*, p. 45.

[117] *Ibid.*, p. 22.

[118] *Ibid.*, pp. 69–71.

[119] *Ibid.*, p. 2.

[120] Augusta I. Barrick, "Morning Meditations," *NEA Journal*, XXXVI (January, 1947), p. 35.

[121] *Ibid.*, p. 35.

[122] A. H. Busker, "An Adventure in Religious Education," *NEA Journal*, XXXV (November, 1946), p. 480.

[123] McKendry, *op. cit.*, p. 204.

[124] Elizabeth Manwell and Sophia L. Fahs, *Consider the Children— How They Grow* (Boston, The Beacon Press, 1946).

[125] Donald E. Super, *The Dynamics of Vocational Adjustment* (New York, Harper & Brothers, 1942), p. 13.

[126] Harry Emerson Fosdick, *On Being a Real Person* (New York, Harper & Brothers, 1943).

[127] Joseph Loth Licbman, *Peace of Mind* (New York, Simon and Schuster, 1946).

[128] Mary Peacock Douglas, "Functions and Standards for a School Library," *The School Executive*, LXIV (December, 1944), p. 51.

[129] Edgar Dale, *Audio-Visual Methods in Teaching* (New York, The Dryden Press, 1946).

[130] L. Harry Strauss and J. H. Kidd, *Look, Listen, and Learn* (New York, Association Press, 1948).

CHAPTER 3

[1] American Council on Education, *Religion and Public Education*. A Report of a Conference Called by the American Council on Education with the Cooperation of the National Conference of Christians and Jews (Princeton, New Jersey, 1944), p. 33.

[2] American Council on Education, *The Relation of Religion to Public Education: The Basic Principles*. A Report by the Committee on Religion and Education (Washington, D. C., American Council on Education, 1947), p. 51.

[3] *Ibid.*, p. 13.

[4] *Ibid.*, p. 20.

[5] Letter from Erdman Harris, Headmaster, Shady Side Academy, Pittsburgh, Pennsylvania, December 24, 1947.

[6] American Council on Education, *The Relation of Religion to Public Education: The Basic Principles*. A Report Prepared by the Committee on Religion and Education (Washington, D. C., American Council on Education, 1947), p. 19.

[7] Paul R. Mort and William S. Vincent, *A Look at Our Schools* (New York, The Ronald Press, 1946), p. 13.

[8] Los Angeles City Schools, *op. cit.*, p. 46.

[9] From *A Cultural History of Education*, by R. Freeman Butts, 1947. Courtesy of McGraw-Hill Book Co., p. 625.

[10] Ps. 19:1.

[11] *The Churchman*, CLXII (January 1, 1948), p. 22.

[12] Letter from Abby A. Sutherland, President, Ogontz Junior College, Ogontz School Post Office, Pennsylvania, December 13, 1947.

[13] Walter Holcomb, "Religion and Education in American Culture" (Unpublished report written for course in Religious Education 288 in Union Theological Seminary, New York City, 1947).

[14] Brubacher (ed.), *op. cit.*, p. 78.

[15] B. Othanel Smith, "Evaluations of *The Relation of Religion to Public Education—The Basic Principles*," *Religious Education*, XLII (May–June, 1947), p. 182. Used by permission of *Religious Education*, 20 West Jackson Boulevard, Chicago 4, Illinois.

[16] Conrad Henry Moehlman, *School and Church: The American Way* (New York, Harper & Brothers, 1944), pp. 103–104.

[17] National Education Association, *The State and Sectarian Education*. Research Bulletin Prepared by the Research Division (Washington, D. C., National Education Association, 1946).

CHAPTER 4

[1] Solomon B. Freehof, "Evaluations of 'The Relation of Religion to Public Education—The Basic Principles,'" *Religious Education*, XLII (May-June, 1947), pp. 164–165. Used by permission of *Religious Education*, 20 West Jackson Boulevard, Chicago 4, Illinois.

[2] American Council on Education, *The Relation of Religion to Public Education: The Basic Principles*, A Report Prepared by the Committee on Religion and Education (Washington, D. C., American Council on Education, 1947), p. 36.

[3] Hook, *op. cit.*, p. 180.

[4] Mort, *op. cit.*, p. 34.

[5] *Ibid.*, p. 37.

[6] *Ibid.*, p. 38.

[7] *Ibid.*, p. 39.

[8] *Ibid.*, p. 42.

[9] Williams, *op. cit.*, pp. 93–113.

[10] National Education Association, *Policies of Education in American Democracy*, Prepared by the Educational Policies Commission (Washington, D. C., National Education Association, 1946), p. 152.

[11] Hughes Mearns, *The Creative Adult* (New York, Doubleday, Doran and Company, 1940), p. 10.

[12] *Ibid.*, p. 2.

[13] American Council on Education, *The Relation of Religion to Public Education: The Basic Principles*, A Report Prepared by the Committee on Religion and Education (Washington, D. C., American Council on Education, 1947), p. 34.

[14] Willis A. Sutton, "Let's Teach Religion in the Public School," *International Journal of Religious Education*, XVII (November, 1940), p. 40.

[15] Letter from Charles Clayton Morrison, Chicago, Illinois, December 3, 1947.

CHAPTER 5

[1] Prudence Bostwick, "Cooperative Action Is One Vital Aspect of Democratic Living," *Educational Administration and Supervision*, XXXIII (October, 1947), p. 361.

[2] Kurt Lewin, "The Dynamics of Group Action," *Educational Leadership*, I (January, 1944), pp. 195–200.

[3] Mort, *op. cit.*, p. 96.

[4] *Ibid.*, pp. 91–248.

[5] American Council on Education, *The Relation of Religion to Public Education: The Basic Principles*, A Report Prepared by the Committee on Religion and Education (Washington, D. C., American Council on Education, 1947), p. vi.

[6] William Clayton Bower, *Church and State in Education* (Chicago, The University of Chicago Press, 1944), p. 4.

[7] Freehof, op. cit., p. 164.

[8] Walter Petitt, "Education and the Autonomous Group," The Journal of Educational Sociology, XIX (May, 1946), p. 530.

[9] Christianity and Crisis, VIII (March 1, 1948), p. 22.

[10] Williams, op. cit.

[11] William Clayton Bower, Church and State in Education (Chicago, The University of Chicago Press, 1944).

[12] American Council on Education, The Relation of Religion to Public Education: The Basic Principles. Report Prepared by the Committee on Religion and Education (Washington, D. C., American Council on Education, 1947).

[13] National Education Association, The State and Sectarian Education, Bulletin Prepared by the Research Division (Washington, D. C., National Education Association, 1946).

[14] Brubacher (ed.), op. cit.

[15] Ernest J. Chave, A Functional Approach to Religious Education (Chicago, The University of Chicago Press, 1947).

[16] Moehlman, op. cit.

[17] Thayer, op. cit.

[18] Cubberley, op. cit.

[19] Butts, op. cit.

[20] R. Bruce Raup, Education and Organized Interests in America (New York, G. P. Putnam's Sons, 1936).

[21] Harrison S. Elliott, The Process of Group Thinking (New York, Association Press, 1928).

[22] Ordway Tead, The Art of Leadership (New York, McGraw-Hill Book Company, 1935).

[23] National Education Association, Leadership at Work. Fifteenth Yearbook, Department of Supervisors and Directors of Instruction (Washington, D. C., National Education Association, 1943).

[24] Horace Mann-Lincoln Institute of School Experimentation, The Teacher's Role in Pupil-Teacher Planning (New York, Bureau of Publications, Teachers College, Columbia University, 1947).

[25] Horace Mann-Lincoln Institute of School Experimentation. Guide to Study and Experimentation in Cooperative Planning in Education (New York, Bureau of Publications, Teachers College, Columbia University, 1947).

[26] Ohio State University, Were We Guinea Pigs? (New York, Henry Holt and Company, 1938).

[27] Julia Weber, My Country School Diary (New York, Harper & Brothers, 1946).

[28] Los Angeles City Schools, op. cit.

[29] Clarence I. Chatto and Alice L. Halligan, *The Story of the Springfield Plan* (New York, Barnes and Noble, Inc., 1945).

[30] James Chrietzberg (ed.), *The Story of Holtville*, Developed by the High School Faculty in Cooperation with the Southern Association Staff Study (Deatsville, Alabama, Holtville High School, 1944).

[31] Theodore Brameld, *Minority Problems in the Public Schools* (New York, Harper & Brothers, 1946).

CHAPTER 6

[1] Mort and Vincent, *op. cit.*, p. 89.

[2] National Education Association, *Planning Postwar Education*, Prepared by the Department of Classroom Teachers and Research Division (Washington, D. C., National Education Association, 1944).

[3] *Survey Graphic*, XXXVI (November, 1947).

[4] Mort and Vincent, *op. cit.*

[5] National Education Association, *Policies for Education in American Democracy*, Prepared by the Educational Policies Commission (Washington, D. C., National Education Association, 1946).

[6] Holcomb, *op. cit.*

[7] Jean Ogden and Jess Ogden, *Small Communities in Action* (New York, Harper & Brothers, 1946).

[8] Theodore Brameld, *Design for America* (New York, Hinds, Hayden and Eldredge, Inc., 1945).

[9] National Education Association, *Education for ALL American Youth*, Prepared by the Educational Policies Commission (Washington, D. C., National Education Association, 1944).

[10] National Education Association, *Spiritual Values in the Elementary School*, Bulletin of the Department of Elementary School Principals (Washington, D. C., National Education Association, September, 1947).

[11] Public Affairs Committee, *Youth and Your Community* (New York, Public Affairs Committee, Inc., 1945).

[12] Margaret O. Koopman, *Utilizing the Local Community* (New York, Hinds, Hayden and Eldredge, Inc., 1946).

[13] Edward G. Olsen (ed.), *School and Community* (New York, Prentice-Hall, Inc., 1945).

[14] Robert L. Sharp, "School Public Relations Via a Community Council," *The American School Board Journal*, CXV (August, 1947).

[15] Olsen (ed.), *op. cit.*, p. 371.

[16] Letter from Edmund deS. Brunner, Professor of Education, Teachers College, Columbia University, New York, November 14, 1947.

[17] McCasland, op. cit.

[18] Lester B. Sands, "A Suggested Approach to Evaluation of Spiritual Values," Spiritual Values in the Elementary School, Bulletin of the Department of Elementary School Principals (Washington, D. C., National Education Association, September, 1947), p. 222.

[19] Ernest M. Ligon, "The Minimum Essentials of Character Education," Religious Education, XXXIX (November-December, 1944), p. 330. Used by permission of Religious Education, 20 West Jackson Boulevard, Chicago 4, Illinois.

[20] Chatto and Halligan, op. cit., pp. 144–148.

[21] George H. Henry, "An Attempt to Measure Ideals," The English Journal, XXXV (November, 1946), pp. 488–489.

[22] Genevieve Bowen, "Evaluation in the Realm of Spiritual Values," Spiritual Values in the Elementary School, Bulletin of the Department of Elementary School Principals (Washington, D. C., National Education Association, September, 1947), pp. 211–213.

[23] Brubacher (ed.), op. cit., p. 84.

[24] Russell Lynes, "Can Private Schools Survive?" Harper's Magazine, CXCVI (January, 1948), pp. 39–48.

[25] U. S. Office of Education, Public Relations for Rural and Village Teachers, Bulletin 1946, No. 16 (Washington, D. C., U. S. Government Printing Office, 1946).

Bibliography

BOOKS

AMERICAN BIBLE SOCIETY. *The Influence of the English Bible upon the English Language and upon English and American Literatures.* New York, American Bible Society.

AMERICAN COUNCIL ON EDUCATION. *Religion and Public Education.* A Report of a Conference Called by the American Council on Education with the Cooperation of the National Conference of Christians and Jews, and Held in Princeton, New Jersey, in 1944. Washington, D.C., American Council on Education, 1944.

AMERICAN COUNCIL ON EDUCATION. *The Relation of Religion to Public Education: The Basic Principles.* A Report Prepared by the Committee on Religion and Education. Washington, D.C., American Council on Education, 1947.

ATTWATER, DONALD. *A Catholic Dictionary.* New York, The Macmillan Company, 1941.

BAINTON, ROLAND H. *The Church of Our Fathers.* New York, Charles Scribner's Sons, 1941.

BAXTER, EDNA M. *How Our Religion Began.* New York, Harper & Brothers, 1939.

BOWER, WILLIAM CLAYTON. *The Living Bible.* New York, Harper & Brothers, 1936.

BOWER, WILLIAM CLAYTON. *Church and State in Education.* Chicago, The University of Chicago Press, 1944.

BOWIE, WALTER R. *The Story of the Bible.* New York, Abingdon Press, 1934.

BOWIE, WALTER R. *Great Men of the Bible.* New York, Harper & Brothers, 1937.

BRADEN, CHARLES SAMUEL. *The World's Religions.* Nashville, The Cokesbury Press, 1939.

BRADY SCHOOL. *Brady School Plan for Character and Citizenship Training.* Manual Prepared by the Brady School Faculty, Detroit, Michigan. Detroit, The Wines Printing Company, 1947.

BRAMELD, THEODORE. *Design for America.* New York, Hinds, Hayden and Eldredge, Inc., 1945.

BRAMELD, THEODORE. *Minority Problems in the Public Schools*. New York, Harper & Brothers, 1946.

BROWNE, LEWIS. *The Graphic Bible*. New York, The Macmillan Company, 1929.

BROWNE, LEWIS. *This Believing World*. New York, The Macmillan Company, 1929.

BROWNE, LEWIS. *The World's Great Scriptures*. New York, The Macmillan Company, 1946.

BRUBACHER, JOHN S. (ed.). *The Public Schools and Spiritual Values*. New York, Harper & Brothers, 1944.

BUTTS, R. FREEMAN. *A Cultural History of Education*. New York, McGraw-Hill Book Company, Inc., 1947.

CALHOUN, ROBERT L. *What Is Man?* New York, Association Press, 1939.

CHASE, MARY ELLEN. *The Bible and the Common Reader*. New York, The Macmillan Company, 1945.

CHATTO, CLARENCE I., and HALLIGAN, ALICE L. *The Story of the Springfield Plan*. New York, Barnes and Noble, Inc., 1945.

CHAVE, ERNEST J. *A Functional Approach to Religious Education*. Chicago, The University of Chicago Press, 1947.

CHRIETZBERG, JAMES (ed.). *The Story of Holtville*. Developed by the High School Faculty in Cooperation with the Southern Association Staff Study. Deatsville, Alabama, Holtville High School, 1944.

COHEN, LENORE. *Bible Tales for Very Young Children*. 2 vols. Cincinnati, The Union of American Hebrew Congregations, 1934, 1936.

CRONBACH, ABRAHAM. *The Bible and Our Social Outlook*. Cincinnati, The Riverdale Press, 1941.

CUBBERLEY, ELLWOOD P. *The Public Education in the United States*. New York, Houghton–Mifflin Company, 1934.

CURTIS, MURIEL STREIBERT. *The Story of the Bible People*. New York, The Macmillan Company, 1942.

DALE, EDGAR. *Audio-Visual Methods in Teaching*. New York, The Dryden Press, 1946.

DAVIDSON, H. MARTIN P. *Good Christian Men*. New York, Charles Scribner's Sons, 1940.

DESJARDINS, LUCILLE. *Our Living Church*. Philadelphia, The Westminster Press, 1936.

DOUGLASS, PAUL, and BRUNNER, EDMUND DES. *The Protestant Church as a Social Institution*. New York, Harper & Brothers, 1935.

EAKIN, MILDRED MOODY. *Getting Acquainted with Jewish Neighbors*. New York, The Macmillan Company, 1945.

EAKIN, FRANK, and EAKIN, MILDRED MOODY. *Let's Think about Our Religion*. New York, The Macmillan Company, 1944.

EASTMAN, FRED (ed.). *Ten One-Act Plays*. Chicago, Willett, Clark and Company, 1937.

ELLIOTT, HARRISON S. *The Process of Group Thinking*. New York, Association Press, 1928.

ELLIOTT, JOHN H. *Building Bridges*. New York, The National Conference of Christians and Jews, 1947.

FAHS, SOPHIA L. *Beginnings of Earth and Sky*. Boston, The Beacon Press, 1937.

FAHS, SOPHIA L. *Jesus, the Carpenter's Son*. Boston, The Beacon Press, 1946.

FAHS, SOPHIA L., and SPOERL, DOROTHY T. *Beginnings of Life and Death*. Boston, The Beacon Press, 1938.

FINKELSTEIN, LOUIS, ELLIOTT, J. ROSS, and BROWN, WILLIAM ADAMS. *The Religions of Democracy*. New York, Devin-Adair Company, 1946.

FITCH, FLORENCE M. *One God: The Ways We Worship Him*. New York, Lothrop, Lee and Shepard, 1944.

FITCH, FLORENCE M. *Their Search for God*. New York, Lothrop, Lee and Shepard, 1947.

FLIGHT, JOHN W. *Moses*. Boston, The Beacon Press, 1942.

FOSDICK, HARRY EMERSON. *The Meaning of Faith*. New York, Association Press, 1917.

FOSDICK, HARRY EMERSON. *On Being a Real Person*. New York, Harper & Brothers, 1943.

GAER, JOSEPH. *How the Great Religions Began*. New York, Robert M. McBride and Company, 1929.

GOODSPEED, EDGAR J. *The Junior Bible*. New York, The Macmillan Company, 1936.

GOODSPEED, EDGAR J. *The Story of the Bible*. Chicago, The University of Chicago Press, 1936.

GOODSPEED, EDGAR J. *How to Read the Bible*. Philadelphia, The John C. Winston Company, 1946.

HAUSER, C. A. *Latent Religious Resources in Public School Education*. Philadelphia, The Heidelberg Press, 1924.

HAUSER, C. A. *Teaching Religion in the Public School*. New York, Round Table Press, 1942.

HAZEN FOUNDATION. "Hazen Books on Religion." Distributed by Association Press, New York.

HEDLEY, GEORGE. *The Christian Heritage in America*. New York, The Macmillan Company, 1947.

HILL, CAROLINE MILES (ed.). *The World's Great Religious Poetry*. New York, The Macmillan Company, 1923.

HILLIS, VERNA. *Martin and Judy*. Vol. I. Boston, The Beacon Press, 1939.

HILLIS, VERNA, and FAHS, SOPHIA L. *Martin and Judy*. Vols. II–III.
Boston, The Beacon Press, 1940, 1943.

HOOK, SIDNEY. *Education for Modern Man*. New York, The Dial
Press, 1946.

HORACE MANN–LINCOLN INSTITUTE OF SCHOOL EXPERIMENTATION.
*Guide to Study and Experimentation in Cooperative Planning in
Education*. New York, Bureau of Publications, Teachers College,
Columbia University, 1947.

HORACE MANN–LINCOLN INSTITUTE OF SCHOOL EXPERIMENTATION.
The Teacher's Role in Pupil–Teacher Planning. New York, Bureau
of Publications, Teacher's College, Columbia University, 1947.

HUME, ROBERT M. *The World's Living Religions*. New York, Charles
Scribner's Sons, 1924.

HYDE, WILLIAM DEWITT. *The Five Great Philosophies*. New York,
The Macmillan Company, 1913.

JACOBUS, M. W., LANE, E. C., and ZENOS, A. C. *A New Standard
Bible Dictionary*. New York, Funk and Wagnalls Company, 1938.

KEAN, CHARLES DUELL. *Christianity and the Cultural Crisis*. New
York, Association Press, 1945.

KLABER, FLORENCE W. *Joseph*. Boston, The Beacon Press, 1941.

KOOPMAN, MARGARET O. *Utilizing the Local Community*. New York,
Hinds, Hayden and Eldredge, Inc., 1946.

LANDIS, BENSON Y. (ed.). *Religion and the Good Society*. New York,
The National Conference of Christians and Jews, 1943.

LANKARD, FRANK GLENN. *The Bible Speaks to Our Generation*. New
York, Oxford University Press, 1941.

LASKI, HAROLD. *Faith, Reason, and Civilization*. New York, The Viking
Press, 1944.

LIEBMAN, JOSEPH LOTH. *Peace of Mind*. New York, Simon and
Schuster, 1946.

LOS ANGELES CITY SCHOOLS. *Moral and Spiritual Values in Education*.
Issued by the Secondary Curriculum Section, but Produced Cooperatively by Many Groups within the Community. Los Angeles, California, City Schools, 1945.

LOUISVILLE PUBLIC SCHOOLS. *Tentative Course of Study, MUSIC,
Junior High Schools*. Issued by the Division of Curriculum and
Research. Louisville, Kentucky, Public Schools, 1947.

MCCASLAND, S. VERNON. *The Bible in Our American Life*. Bridge-
water, Virginia, Virginia Council of Churches, Inc.

MACMURRAY, JOHN. *The Structure of Religious Experience*. New
Haven, The Yale University Press, 1936.

MANWELL, ELIZABETH, and FAHS, SOPHIA L. *Consider the Children—
How They Grow*. Boston, The Beacon Press, 1946.

MANWELL, REGINALD, and FAHS, SOPHIA L. *The Church across the Street.* Boston, The Beacon Press, 1947.

MAUS, CYNTHIA PEARL. *Christ and the Fine Arts.* New York, Harper & Brothers, 1938.

MEARNS, HUGHES. *The Creative Adult.* New York, Doubleday, Doran and Company, 1940.

MOEHLMAN, CONRAD HENRY. *School and Church: The American Way.* New York, Harper & Brothers, 1944.

MONTGOMERY COUNTY SCHOOLS. *Data Bulletin: Tenth Grade Social Studies.* Prepared by a County Committee Assisted by Staff Members of the U.S. Office of Education. Montgomery County, Rockville, Maryland, Public Schools, 1941.

MORT, PAUL R. *Principles of School Administration.* New York, Mc-Graw-Hill Book Company, 1946.

MORT, PAUL R., and VINCENT, WILLIAM S. *A Look at Our Schools.* New York, The Ronald Press, 1946.

MORTON, H. V. *Women of the Bible.* New York, Dodd, Mead and Company, 1941.

MUNKRES, ALBERTA. *Which Way for Our Children?* New York, Charles Scribner's Sons, 1936.

NATIONAL EDUCATION ASSOCIATION. *Leadership at Work.* Fifteenth Yearbook, Department of Supervisors and Directors of Instruction. Washington, D.C., National Education Association, 1943.

NATIONAL EDUCATION ASSOCIATION. *Education for ALL American Youth.* Prepared by the Educational Policies Commission. Washington, D.C., National Education Association, 1944.

NATIONAL EDUCATION ASSOCIATION. *Personal Growth Leaflets.* Leaflets Published for Sale at Cost by the Hugh Birch–Horace Mann Fund. Washington, D.C., National Education Association.

NATIONAL EDUCATION ASSOCIATION. *Planning Postwar Education.* Prepared by the Department of Classroom Teachers and Research Division. Washington, D.C., National Education Association, 1944.

NATIONAL EDUCATION ASSOCIATION. *Policies for Education in American Democracy.* Prepared by the Educational Policies Commission. Washington, D.C., National Education Association, 1946.

NATIONAL EDUCATION ASSOCIATION. *The State and Sectarian Education.* Bulletin Prepared by the Research Division. Washington, D.C., National Education Association, 1946.

NATIONAL EDUCATION ASSOCIATION. *Spiritual Values in the Elementary School.* Bulletin of the Department of Elementary School Principals. Washington, D.C., National Education Association, September, 1947.

NELSON, LAWRENCE E. *Our Roving Bible.* New York, Abingdon–Cokesbury Press, 1945.

OGDEN, JEAN, and OGDEN, JESS. *Small Communities in Action*. New York, Harper & Brothers, 1946.

OHIO STATE UNIVERSITY. *Were We Guinea Pigs?* New York, Henry Holt and Company, 1938.

OLSEN, EDWARD G. (ed.). *School and Community*. New York, Prentice–Hall, Inc., 1945.

OWEN, RALPH D. *Learning Religion from Famous Americans*. New York, The Macmillan Company, 1927.

PHELPS, WILLIAM LYON. *Human Nature in the Bible*. New York, Charles Scribner's Sons, 1922.

PUBLIC AFFAIRS COMMITTEE. *Youth and Your Community*. New York, Public Affairs Committee, Inc., 1945.

RAUP, R. BRUCE. *Education and Organized Interests in America*. New York, G. P. Putnam's Sons, 1936.

SHERRILL, LEWIS JOSEPH. *The Opening Doors of Childhood*. New York, The Macmillan Company, 1939.

SMITHER, ETHEL L. *A Picture Book of Palestine*. New York, Abingdon–Cokesbury Press, 1947.

STEINBERG, MILTON. *Basic Judaism*. New York, Harcourt, Brace and Company, 1947.

STEVENS, BERTHA. *Child and Universe*. New York, The John Day Company, 1931.

STEVENS, BERTHA. *How Miracles Abound*. Boston, The Beacon Press, 1941.

STRAUSS, L. HARRY, and KIDD, J. R. *Look, Listen, and Learn*. New York, Association Press, 1948.

STRAUSS, ROGER WILLIAMS. *Religious Liberty and Democracy*. New York, Willett, Clark and Company, 1939.

SUPER, DONALD E. *The Dynamics of Vocational Adjustment*. New York, Harper & Brothers, 1942.

SUPREME COURT OF THE UNITED STATES. *People of the State of Illinois ex. rel. Vashti McCollum, Appellant, v. Board of Education of School District No. 71, Champaign County, Illinois et al.: Appeal from the Supreme Court of the State of Illinois* (No. 90, October Term, 1947–March 8, 1948).

SWEET, WILLIAM W. *The Story of Religion in America*. New York, Harper & Brothers, 1939.

SYPHERD, WILBUR OWEN. *The Book of Books*. New York, Alfred A. Knopf Company, 1944.

TEAD, ORDWAY. *The Art of Leadership*. New York, McGraw–Hill Book Company, 1935.

THAYER, V. T. *Religion in Public Education*. New York, The Viking Press, 1947.

UNITED CHRISTIAN YOUTH MOVEMENT. *Christian Youth and Interfaith Cooperation.* Chicago, The United Christian Youth Movement, 1944.

UNITED STATES OFFICE OF EDUCATION. *Public Relations for Rural and Village Teachers.* Bulletin 1946, No. 16. Washington, D.C., The United States Government Printing Office, 1946.

VAN LOON, HENDRICK. *The Story of the Bible.* New York, Boni and Liveright, 1923.

WALLACE, ARCHER. *The Religious Faith of Great Men.* New York, Round Table Press, 1941.

WEBER, JULIA. *My Country School Diary.* New York, Harper & Brothers, 1946.

WICKENDEN, ARTHUR C. *Youth Looks at Religion.* New York, Harper & Brothers, 1939.

WILLIAMS, J. PAUL. *The New Education and Religion.* New York, Association Press, 1946.

ARTICLES

BAKER, HAROLD V. "Spiritual Values Give Life Its Highest Meaning," *NEA Journal,* XXXVI (December, 1947), 628-629.

BARRICK, AUGUSTA I. "Morning Meditations," *NEA Journal,* XXXVI (January, 1947), 35.

BASINGER, ANNE LLOYD. "Religion at Brearley," *The Brearley Bulletin,* New York, N.Y., XX (December, 1944), 10.

BOSTWICK, PRUDENCE. "Cooperative Action Is One Vital Aspect of Democratic Living," *Educational Administration and Supervision,* XXXIII (October, 1947), 361-364.

BOWEN, GENEVIEVE. "Evaluation in the Realm of Spiritual Values," *Spiritual Values in the Elementary Schools,* Bulletin of the Department of Elementary School Principals (Washington, D.C., National Education Association, September, 1947), 211-213.

BUEKER, A. H. "An Adventure in Religious Education," *NEA Journal,* XXXV (November, 1946), 480.

"CAROLS," *The Churchman,* CLXII (January 1, 1948), 22.

CHILDS, JOHN L. "Spiritual Values in Public Education," *Teachers College Record,* XLVIII (March, 1947), 367-373.

"CHURCH AND STATE—SOME CURRENT ISSUES," *Information Service,* Federal Council of the Churches of Christ in America, XX (November 15, 1941).

DESJARDINS, LUCILLE, "Resources for Religious Education," *The International Journal of Religious Education,* XI (October, 1934), 22-23.

DIMOCK, HEDLEY S. "The Character Education of the Adolescent," *Religious Education*, XLII (July–August, 1947), 234–242.

DOUGLAS, MARY PEACOCK, "Functions and Standards of a School Library," *The School Executive*, LXIV (December, 1944), 50–52.

FOSDICK, HARRY EMERSON, "Shall American School Children Be Religiously Illiterate?" *School and Society*, LXVI (November 29, 1947), 401–406.

FREEHOF, SOLOMON B. "Evaluations of The Relation of Religion to Public Education: The Basic Principles." *Religious Education*, XLII (May–June, 1947), 163–165.

GANS, ROMA. "Teachers Appraise Supervision and Administration," *Education*, (December, 1946), 217–222.

GLENN, C. LESLIE. "Why I Read the Bible," *The Atlantic Monthly*, CLXXVI (September, 1945), 63–66.

HENRY, GEORGE H. "An Attempt to Measure Ideals," *The English Journal*, XXXV (November, 1946), 488–489.

HIGH, STANLEY. "Our Schools Need More Than Money," *The Reader's Digest*, XXVI (December, 1947), 15–17.

KELIHER, ALICE V. "No Monopoly on Leadership," *Educational Leadership*, IV (January, 1947), 214–217.

LEWIN, KURT. "The Dynamics of Group Action," *Educational Leadership*, I (January, 1944), 195–200.

LIGON, ERNEST M. "The Minimum Essentials of Character Education," *Religious Education*, XXXIX (November–December, 1944), 321–335.

LINDEMAN, EDUARD C. "The Enduring Goal," *Survey Graphic*, XXXVI (November, 1947), 637–640.

LINDEMAN, EDUARD C. "Sources of Value for Modern Man," *Religious Education*, XLIII (September–October, 1947), 285–290.

LYNES, RUSSELL. "Can the Private Schools Survive?" *Harper's Magazine*, CXCVI (January, 1948), 39–48.

McKENDRY, JAMES B. "Correlation of Week-Day Religious Education with the Public School Program," *Religious Education*, XLII (July–August, 1947), 202–207.

MORRISON, CHARLES CLAYTON. "The Inner Citadel of Democracy," *The Christian Century*, XLIII (May 7, 1941), 652–654.

MORRISON, CHARLES CLAYTON. "Protestantism and the Public Schools," *The Christian Century*, XLIII (April 17, 1946), 490–493.

NALL, FRANCES. "Correlating the Curriculum of the Church and School," *Religious Education*, XXXVII (September–October, 1942), 287–293.

NIEBUHR, REINHOLD. "Our Relations to Catholicism," *Christianity and Crisis*, VIII (September 15, 1947), 5–7.

NIEBUHR, REINHOLD. "The Impact of Protestantism Today," *The Atlantic Monthly*, CLXXXI (February, 1948), 57–62.

PETTIT, WALTER. "Education and the Autonomous Group," *The Journal of Educational Sociology*, XIX (May, 1946), 529–533.

"ROCHESTER INTER-FAITH COMMITTEE STATEMENT," *Christianity and Crisis*, VIII (March 1, 1948), 22.

SANDS, LESTER B. "A Suggested Approach to Evaluation of Spiritual Values," *Spiritual Values in the Elementary School*, Bulletin of the Department of Elementary School Principals (Washington, D.C., National Education Association, September, 1947), 222–226.

SHARP, ROBERT L. "School Public Relations Via a Community Council," *The American School Board Journal*, CXV (August, 1947), 371–372.

SMITH, B. OTHANEL. "Evaluations of *The Relation of Religion to Public Education: The Basic Principles*," *Religious Education*, XLII (May–June, 1947), 181–186.

SUTTON, WILLIS A. "Let's Teach Religion in the Public Schools," *The International Journal of Religious Education*, XVII (November, 1940), 12, 40.

TROYER, WILLIAM LEWIS. "Christian Nurture and Recent Social Science Investigation," *Religious Education*, XLII (November–December, 1947), 351–356.

UNPUBLISHED MATERIAL

BROOKS SCHOOL. Letter from Frank D. Ashburn, Headmaster, Brooks School, North Andover, Massachusetts, December 14, 1947.

HOLCOMB, WALTER. "Religion and Education in American Culture." Unpublished report written for course in Religious Education 288 in Union Theological Seminary, New York City, 1947.

HOWSON, HOWARD J. "The Curricular Approach to Religious Prejudice." Unpublished report of a study conducted for the American Conference of Christians and Jews, 1942–43. (Available in Vassar College Library.)

LOUISVILLE PUBLIC SCHOOLS. Letter from Robert Allen, Assistant in Curriculum, Public Schools, Louisville, Kentucky, January 19, 1948.

MORRISON, CHARLES CLAYTON. Personal letter received in response to request for criticism of project outline, December 3, 1947.

OGONTZ JUNIOR COLLEGE. Letter from Abby A. Sutherland, President, Ogontz Junior College, Ogontz School Post Office, Pennsylvania, December 13, 1947.

SHADY SIDE ACADEMY. Letter from Erdman Harris, Headmaster, Shady Side Academy, Pittsburgh, Pennsylvania, December 24, 1947.

TEACHERS COLLEGE, COLUMBIA UNIVERSITY. Letter from Edmund
deS. Brunner, Professor of Education, Teachers College, Columbia
University, New York City, November 14, 1947.

MISCELLANEOUS

AMERICAN BIBLE SOCIETY. "Forty Favorite Chapters in Your Bible."
A selected list of chapters for daily Bible reading. New York,
American Bible Society.

THE CONSTITUTION OF THE UNITED STATES. Amendments to the Constitution: Articles I, XIV.

GEORGE SCHOOL. "Religion at George School," George School Bulletin, Bucks County, Pennsylvania, March, 1947.

OXNAM, G. BROMLEY, et al. "Are We Losing Our Moral Standards?"
Town Meeting, XIII (February 24, 1948).

Survey Graphic, XXXVI (November, 1947). Special issue on the subject "Calling America: Education for Our Time."

Index